W9-BYU-323

FEEDING THE PLANET:
Environmental Protection through
Sustainable Agriculture

DISCARDED

X

Around the world nearly one billion people suffer from malnutrition. Many of them die each year from starvation, and yet the human population continues to grow unabated. The biosphere and the climate are being seriously threatened and agricultural productivity has stagnated, especially in areas where hunger prevails. Well-fed populations in industrialized countries are particularly called upon to act rapidly and effectively. Klaus Hahlbrock advocates a drastic and immediate change in our attitude towards nature and towards our own species. Absolute priority must be given to the preservation of a rich and viable biosphere for all living creatures, including ourselves.

Klaus Hahlbrock, professor of biochemistry, served as a director at the Max Planck Institute for Plant Breeding Research and as vice president of the Max Planck Society.

Our addresses on the Internet:
www.the-sustainability-project.com
www.forum-fuer-verantwortung.de
[English version available]

HC
79
.E5
H31413
2009

FEEDING THE PLANET:
Environmental Protection
through Sustainable Agriculture

KLAUS HAHLBROCK

DISCARDED

Translated by David Skogley

Klaus Wiegandt, General Editor

HAUS PUBLISHING

Shelton State Libraries
Shelton State Community College

First published in Great Britain in 2009 by
Haus Publishing Ltd
70 Cadogan Place
London SW1X 9AH
www.hauspublishing.com

Originally published as: *Kann unsere Erde die Menschen noch ernähren?*
Bevölkerungsexplosion – Umwelt – Gentechnik by Klaus Hahlbrock

Copyright © 2007 Fischer Taschenbuch Verlag in der S. Fischer Verlag
GmbH, Frankfurt am Main

English translation copyright © David Skogley 2009

The moral right of the author has been asserted

A CIP catalogue record for this book
is available from the British Library

ISBN 978-1-906598-11-2

Typeset in Sabon by MacGuru Ltd
Printed in Dubai by Oriental Press

CONDITIONS OF SALE
All rights reserved. No part of this publication may be reproduced,
stored in a retrieval system, or transmitted in any form or by any means,
electronic, mechanical, photocopying, recording or otherwise, without the
prior permission of the publisher.

This book is sold subject to the condition that it shall not, by way of trade
or otherwise, be lent, re-sold, hired out or otherwise circulated without
the publisher's prior consent in any form of binding or cover other than
that in which it is published and without a similar condition including this
condition being imposed on the subsequent purchaser.

Mixed Sources
Product group from well-managed
forests and other controlled sources
www.fsc.org Cert no. CU-COC-809367
© 1996 Forest Stewardship Council

Haus Publishing believes in the importance of a
sustainable future for our planet. This book is
printed on paper produced in accordance with the
standards of sustainability set out and monitored by
the FSC. The printer holds chain of custody.

Dedicated
to the memory of
my father

Hans Hahlbrock
(1911–1943)

Contents

Editor's Foreword

Sales of the German-language edition of this series have exceeded all expectations. The positive media response has been encouraging, too. Both of these positive responses demonstrate that the series addresses the right topics in a language that is easily understood by the general reader. The combination of thematic breadth and scientifically astute, yet generally accessible writing, is particularly important as I believe it to be a vital prerequisite for smoothing the way to a sustainable society by turning knowledge into action. After all, I am not a scientist myself; my background is in business.

A few months ago, shortly after the first volumes had been published, we received suggestions from neighboring countries in Europe recommending that an English-language edition would reach a far larger readership. Books dealing with global challenges, they said, require global action brought about by informed debate amongst as large an audience as possible. When delegates from India, China, and Pakistan voiced similar concerns at an international conference my mind was made up. Dedicated individuals such as Lester R. Brown and Jonathan Porritt deserve credit for bringing the concept of sustainability to the attention of the general public, I am convinced that this series can give the discourse about sustainability something new.

Two years have passed since I wrote the foreword to the initial German edition. During this time, unsustainable developments on our planet have come to our attention in ever more dramatic ways. The price of oil has nearly tripled; the value of industrial metals has risen exponentially and, quite unexpectedly, the costs of staple foods such as corn, rice, and wheat have reached all-time highs. Around the globe, people are increasingly concerned that the pressure caused by these drastic price increases will lead to serious destabilization in China, India, Indonesia, Vietnam, and Malaysia, the world's key developing regions.

The frequency and intensity of natural disasters brought on by global warming has continued to increase. Many regions of our Earth are experiencing prolonged droughts, with subsequent shortages of drinking water and the destruction of entire harvests. In other parts of the world, typhoons and hurricanes are causing massive flooding and inflicting immeasurable suffering.

The turbulence in the world's financial markets, triggered by the US sub-prime mortgage crisis, has only added to these woes. It has affected every country and made clear just how unscrupulous and sometimes irresponsible speculation has become in today's financial world. The expectation of exorbitant short-term rates of return on capital investments led to complex and obscure financial engineering. Coupled with a reckless willingness to take risks everyone involved seemingly lost track of the situation. How else can blue chip companies incur multi-billion dollar losses? If central banks had not come to the rescue with dramatic steps to back up their currencies, the world's economy would have collapsed. It was only in these circumstances that the use of public monies could be justified. It is therefore imperative to prevent a repeat of speculation with short-term capital on such a gigantic scale.

Taken together, these developments have at least significantly improved the readiness for a debate on sustainability. Many more are now aware that our wasteful use of natural resources and energy have serious consequences, and not only for future generations.

Two years ago, who would have dared to hope that WalMart, the world's largest retailer, would initiate a dialog about sustainability with its customers and promise to put the results into practice? Who would have considered it possible that CNN would start a series "Going Green?" Every day, more and more businesses worldwide announce that they are putting the topic of sustainability at the core of their strategic considerations. Let us use this momentum to try and make sure that these positive developments are not a flash in the pan, but a solid part of our necessary discourse within civic society.

However, we cannot achieve sustainable development through a multitude of individual adjustments. We are facing the challenge of critical fundamental questioning of our lifestyle and consumption and patterns of production. We must grapple with the complexity of the entire earth system in a forward-looking and precautionary manner, and not focus solely on topics such as energy and climate change.

The authors of these twelve books examine the consequences of our destructive interference in the Earth ecosystem from different perspectives. They point out that we still have plenty of opportunities to shape a sustainable future. If we want to achieve this, however, it is imperative that we use the information we have as a basis for systematic action, guided by the principles of sustainable development. If the step from knowledge to action is not only to be taken, but also to succeed, we need to offer comprehensive education to all, with the foundation in early childhood. The central issues of the future must be anchored firmly in school curricula, and no university student should be permitted to graduate without having completed a general course on sustainable development. Everyday opportunities for action must be made clear to us all – young and old. Only then can we begin to think critically about our lifestyles and make positive changes in the direction of sustainability. We need to show the business community the way to sustainable development via a responsible attitude to consumption, and become active within our sphere of influence as opinion leaders.

For this reason, my foundation *Forum für Verantwortung*, the ASKO EUROPA-FOUNDATION, and the European Academy Otzenhausen have joined forces to produce educational materials on the future of the Earth to accompany the twelve books developed at the renowned Wuppertal Institute for Climate, Environment and Energy. We are setting up an extensive program of seminars, and the initial results are very promising. The success of our initiative "Encouraging Sustainability," which has now been awarded the status of an official project of the UN Decade "Education for Sustainable Development," confirms the public's great interest in, and demand for, well-founded information.

I would like to thank the authors for their additional effort to update all their information and put the contents of their original volumes in a more global context. My special thanks goes to the translators, who submitted themselves to a strict timetable, and to Annette Maas for coordinating the Sustainability Project. I am grateful for the expert editorial advice of Amy Irvine and the Haus Publishing editorial team for not losing track of the "3600-page-work."

Taking Action — Out of Insight and Responsibility

"We were on our way to becoming gods, supreme beings who could create a second world, using the natural world only as building blocks for our new creation."

This warning by the psychoanalyst and social philosopher Erich Fromm is to be found in *To Have or to Be?* (1976). It aptly expresses the dilemma in which we find ourselves as a result of our scientific-technical orientation.

The original intention of submitting to nature in order to make use of it ("knowledge is power") evolved into subjugating nature in order to exploit it. We have left the earlier successful path with its many advances and are now on the wrong track, a path of danger with incalculable risks. The greatest danger stems from the unshakable faith of the overwhelming majority of politicians and business leaders in unlimited economic growth which, together with limitless technological innovation, is supposed to provide solutions to all the challenges of the present and the future.

For decades now, scientists have been warning of this collision course with nature. As early as 1983, the United Nations founded the World Commission on Environment and Development which published the Brundtland Report in 1987. Under the title *Our Common Future*, it presented a concept that could save mankind from catastrophe and help to find the way back to a responsible way of life, the concept of long-term environmentally sustainable use of resources. "Sustainability," as used in the Brundtland Report, means "development that meets the needs of the present without compromising the ability of future generations to meet their own needs."

Despite many efforts, this guiding principle for ecologically, economically, and socially sustainable action has unfortunately not yet become the reality it can, indeed must, become. I believe the reason for this is that civil societies have not yet been sufficiently informed and mobilized.

Forum für Verantwortung

Against this background, and in the light of ever more warnings and scientific results, I decided to take on a societal responsibility with my foundation. I would like to contribute to the expansion of public discourse about sustainable development which is absolutely essential. It is my desire to provide a large number of people with facts and contextual knowledge on the subject of sustainability, and to show alternative options for future action.

After all, the principle of "sustainable development" alone is insufficient to change current patterns of living and economic practices. It does provide some orientation, but it has to be negotiated in concrete terms within society and then implemented in patterns of behavior. A democratic society seriously seeking to reorient itself towards future viability must rely on critical, creative individuals capable of both discussion and action. For this reason, life-long learning, from childhood to old age, is a necessary precondition for realizing sustainable development. The practical implementation of the ecological, economic, and social goals of a sustainability strategy in economic policy requires people able to reflect, innovate and recognize potentials for structural change and learn to use them in the best interests of society.

It is not enough for individuals to be merely "concerned." On the contrary, it is necessary to understand the scientific background and interconnections in order to have access to them and be able to develop them in discussions that lead in the right direction. Only in this way can the ability to make appropriate judgments emerge, and this is a prerequisite for responsible action.

The essential condition for this is presentation of both the facts and the theories within whose framework possible courses of action are visible in a manner that is both appropriate to the subject matter and comprehensible. Then, people will be able to use them to guide their personal behavior.

In order to move towards this goal, I asked renowned scientists to present in a generally understandable way the state of research and the possible options on twelve important topics in the area of sustainable development in the series "*Forum für Verantwortung.*" All those involved in this project are in agreement that there is no alternative to a united path of all societies towards sustainability:

- *Our Planet: How Much More Can Earth Take?* (Jill Jäger)
- *Energy: The World's Race for Resources in the 21st Century* (Hermann-Joseph Wagner)
- *Our Threatened Oceans* (Stefan Rahmstorf and Katherine Richardson)
- *Water Resources: Efficient, Sustainable and Equitable Use* (Wolfram Mauser)
- *The Earth: Natural Resources and Human Intervention* (Friedrich Schmidt-Bleek)
- *Overcrowded World? Global Population and International Migration* (Rainer Münz and Albert F. Reiterer)
- *Feeding the Planet: Environmental Protection through Sustainable Agriculture* (Klaus Hahlbrock)
- *Costing the Earth? Perspectives on Sustainable Development* (Bernd Meyer)
- *The New Plagues: Pandemics and Poverty in a Globalized World* (Stefan Kaufmann)

- *Climate Change: The Point of No Return* (Mojib Latif)
- *The Demise of Diversity: Loss and Extinction* (Josef H Reichholf)
- *Building a New World Order: Sustainable Policies for the Future* (Harald Müller)

The public debate

What gives me the courage to carry out this project and the optimism that I will reach civil societies in this way, and possibly provide an impetus for change?

For one thing, I have observed that, because of the number and severity of natural disasters in recent years, people have become more sensitive concerning questions of how we treat the Earth. For another, there are scarcely any books on the market that cover in language comprehensible to civil society the broad spectrum of comprehensive sustainable development in an integrated manner.

When I began to structure my ideas and the prerequisites for a public discourse on sustainability in 2004, I could not foresee that by the time the first books of the series were published, the general public would have come to perceive at least climate change and energy as topics of great concern. I believe this occurred especially as a result of the following events:

First, the United States witnessed the devastation of New Orleans in August 2005 by Hurricane Katrina, and the anarchy following in the wake of this disaster.

Second, in 2006, Al Gore began his information campaign on climate change and wastage of energy, culminating in his film *An Inconvenient Truth*, which has made an impression on a wide audience of all age groups around the world.

Third, the 700-page Stern Report, commissioned by the British government, published in 2007 by the former Chief Economist of the World Bank Nicholas Stern in collaboration with other economists, was a wake-up call for politicians and business leaders alike. This report makes clear how extensive the damage to the global economy will be if we continue with "business as usual" and do not take vigorous steps to halt climate change. At the same time, the report demonstrates that we could finance countermeasures for just one-tenth of the cost of the probable damage, and could limit average global warming to 2° C – if we only took action.

Fourth, the most recent IPCC report, published in early 2007, was met by especially intense media interest, and therefore also received considerable public attention. It laid bare as never before how serious the situation is, and called for drastic action against climate change.

Last, but not least, the exceptional commitment of a number of billionaires such as Bill Gates, Warren Buffett, George Soros, and Richard Branson as well as Bill Clinton's work to "save the world" is impressing people around the globe and deserves mention here.

An important task for the authors of our twelve-volume series was to provide appropriate steps towards sustainable development in their particular subject area. In this context, we must always be aware that successful transition to this type of economic, ecological, and social development on our planet cannot succeed immediately, but will require many decades. Today, there are still no sure formulae for the most successful long-term path. A large number of scientists and even more innovative entrepreneurs and managers will have to use their creativity and dynamism to solve the great challenges. Nonetheless, even today, we can discern the first clear goals we must reach in order to avert a looming catastrophe. And billions of consumers around the world can use their daily purchasing decisions to help both ease and significantly accelerate the economy's transition to sustainable development – provided the political framework is there. In addition, from a global perspective, billions of citizens have the opportunity to mark out the political "guide rails" in a democratic way via their parliaments.

The most important insight currently shared by the scientific, political, and economic communities is that our resource-intensive Western model of prosperity (enjoyed today by one billion people) cannot be extended to another five billion or, by 2050, at least eight billion people. That would go far beyond the biophysical capacity of the planet. This realization is not in dispute. At issue, however, are the consequences we need to draw from it.

If we want to avoid serious conflicts between nations, the industrialized countries must reduce their consumption of resources by more than the developing and threshold countries increase theirs. In the future, all countries must achieve the same level of consumption. Only then will we be able to create the necessary ecological room for maneuver in order to ensure an appropriate level of prosperity for developing and threshold countries.

To avoid a dramatic loss of prosperity in the West during this long-term process of adaptation, the transition from high to low resource use, that is, to an ecological market economy, must be set in motion quickly.

On the other hand, the threshold and developing countries must commit themselves to getting their population growth under control within the foreseeable future. The twenty-year Programme of Action adopted by the United Nations International Conference on Population and Development in Cairo in 1994 must be implemented with stronger support from the industrialized nations.

If humankind does not succeed in drastically improving resource and energy efficiency and reducing population growth in a sustainable manner – we should remind ourselves of the United Nations forecast that population growth will come to a halt only at the end of this century, with a world population of eleven to twelve billion – then we run the real risk of developing eco-dictatorships. In the words of Ernst Ulrich von Weizsäcker: "States will be sorely tempted to ration limited resources, to micromanage economic activity, and in the interest of the environment to specify from above what citizens may or may not do. 'Quality-of-life' experts might define in an authoritarian way what kind of needs people are permitted to satisfy." (*Earth Politics*, 1989, in English translation: 1994).

It is time

It is time for us to take stock in a fundamental and critical way. We, the public, must decide what kind of future we want. Progress and quality of life is not dependent on year-by-year growth in per capita income alone, nor do we need inexorably growing amounts of goods to satisfy our needs. The short-term goals of our economy, such as maximizing profits and accumulating capital, are major obstacles to sustainable development. We should go back to a more decentralized economy and reduce world trade and the waste of energy associated with it in a targeted fashion. If resources and energy were to cost their "true" prices, the global process of rationalization and labor displacement will be reversed, because cost pressure will be shifted to the areas of materials and energy.

The path to sustainability requires enormous technological innovations. But not everything that is technologically possible has to be put into practice. We should not strive to place all areas of our lives under the dictates of the economic system. Making justice and fairness a reality for everyone is not only a moral and ethical imperative, but is also the most important means of securing world peace in the long term. For this reason, it is essential to place the political relationship between states and peoples on a new basis, a basis with which everyone can identify, not only the most powerful. Without common principles of global governance, sustainability cannot become a reality in any of the fields discussed in this series.

And finally, we must ask whether we humans have the right to reproduce to such an extent that we may reach a population of eleven to twelve billion by the end of this century, laying claim to every square centimeter of our Earth and restricting and destroying the habitats and way of life of all other species to an ever greater degree.

Our future is not predetermined. We ourselves shape it by our actions. We can continue as before, but if we do so, we will put ourselves in the biophysical straitjacket of nature, with possibly disastrous political implications, by the middle of this century. But we also have the opportunity to create a fairer and more viable future for ourselves and for future generations. This requires the commitment of everyone on our planet.

Klaus Wiegandt
Summer 2008

This contribution to the series *Forum für Verantwortung* is a completely revised and thoroughly updated version of a book which first appeared under the same title (in German) 15 years ago. Since that time the question of how to feed the people on this planet in a sustainable manner despite persistent population growth and increasing environmental destruction has become even more dramatic. The imbalance between hunger and excess, poverty and wealth, and the overexploitation of resources and ecological stability is becoming larger and larger.

Fifteen years ago we were concerned with the question of whether the newly arising technique of plant genetic engineering would play a role in solving existing breeding problems and whether its application could be ethically and biologically justified. In the meantime genetically engineered plants have been grown in more than a dozen non-European industrial and developing countries in a total area equal to twice the size of France. According to initial analyses, small-scale farmers – particularly in developing countries – have profited in economic terms, while the ecological benefit of employing less environmentally damaging pesticides has been considerable.

In Europe and some other parts of the world this development has scarcely been noted. Thus it is one of the main themes in the present version of this book. The rapidly increasing global threats to agricultural productivity are also dealt with in more detail. New central topics of interest include the continuing destruction of our environment, as well as hunger and poverty in connection with the unabated growth in population in developing countries.

Once again colleagues from related fields have generously provided their expert advice as well as references and images. Thanks are due to Dorothea Bartels, Peter Beyer, Hartwig Geiger, Dennis Gonsalves, Jorge Mayer, Matin Qaim, Wolfgang Schuchert, Walter Schug and Günther Strittmatter. I am especially grateful to Klaus Wiegandt and his foundation *Forum für Verantwortung* for the conception, critical assistance and generous sponsorship of this series of books, as well as to Ernst Peter Fischer as a committed co-publisher and Ulrike Holler as a helpful editor.

Introduction

"Our world has become small" in a time of increasingly rapid and frequent flight connections and high-speed communication between the continents. In our new technology-based metaphorical language we have become used to talking about "Spaceship Earth." We have begun to realize the extent to which we are all "in the same boat."

It has started to get crowded in this boat, or spaceship. The number of passengers is increasing although stores of food are in short supply and waste is increasing at an alarming rate. There aren't even enough scraps left over from first class to satisfy all the rest for very long. We need a fundamental change of course which limits the number of passengers and guarantees healthy and sustainable living conditions for all. And yet, we continue to run at full steam ahead and a change in course is seldom a tight curve. The faster the trip, the wider is the curve – in spite of all the required impatience.

The only solution I see is to end the growth of the human population very quickly in the tightest curve possible. The same also applies to the overuse of our biosphere as well as the social and economic imbalances within and between the various countries. Our consciousness of these problems should be sharpened enough by now to steer this new course in an unswerving manner.

Everyone has to contribute in his or her own way. Agriculture must also make a great effort while playing its part in this new course. The priority, however, must be a limit on population growth in order to make System Earth tolerable for everyone.

For this reason, I will base the following on an important pre-condition: every person has an equal right to exist, now and in the future, and thus has an equal right to the provision of food. I am aware that this demand will have difficult consequences if put into practice. It not only requires a human imperative for solidarity, care and sharing. It implies, moreover, that if there is an unequal division of food those that live below the subsistence level will attempt to claim what they are entitled to – war not being excluded. Indeed we are all sitting in one boat, and we all have every reason to choose the course judiciously.

The exact course we decide upon must be primarily oriented toward our threatened basic needs and, at the same time, focus on our responsibility for future generations. First of all, this requires an unbiased determination of our present situation. Then we have to determine the means at our disposal and decide on how they can be used to solve existing problems. Suitable technical wherewithal should make it possible to set a course, but they should not determine such a course a priori. With regard to human nourishment, this has in particular recently involved the application of genetic engineering.

Insofar as genetic engineering is considered to be an innova-tive tool in plant breeding, there remains the difficult task of its ethical evaluation. The technology itself was developed within just a few decades. However, its ethical evaluation is only possi-ble against the backdrop of a long and complex interdependence between humans and their environment.

The chapters of this book are organized accordingly. The current position of contemporary human beings and their relationship to the supporting biosphere is determined by presenting several fundamental facts and prerequisites followed, in turn, by a brief historical outline of the development of agriculture and human ways of life.

In the main part of the book, individual chapters deal with the breeding of agricultural crops, the present situation and anticipated innovative potential of genetic engineering, as well as the actual core question of how our Earth can continue to provide us with enough food. On the one hand, I wish to contribute to the body of required factual information as much as possible and, on the other, create a broad basis with which to conduct an ethical evaluation and draw practical conclusions. In order to separate objective information from individual judgment in a perceptible manner this book concludes with a personal afterword. This serves to remind us that each individual is called upon to state his or her opinion and contribute to a sustainable future – no matter where they stand.

In order to keep the subject of the book within a reasonable framework I have largely restricted myself to discussing agricultural crops as the primary basis of food for humans and animals. However, unless expressly noted, this limitation shall have no impact on the discussion of fundamental questions.

For the most part I have avoided using tables and statistics. In my experience they only serve to distract readers from the main point. Where figures are used at all, they are intended to underscore a trend rather than provide absolute values. Disagreements about figures, statistics and forecasts, and insufficiently founded hypotheses have done more damage than good, especially where the complex topics of environmental protection and the security of food supplies are concerned.

More important than the exactness of *absolute figures* is the *absolute will* to preserve or restore a diverse, sustainable and viable biosphere, clean soil and water, and a healthy climate as a secure basis of life to as great an extent as possible. I assume this common goal to be self-evident, without justifying each individual point. This will determine the new course.

1 Human Population and Ecological Consequences

The history of mankind is at a turning point. Those of us now alive must decide about how we want to end the unabated growth of the human population and the concurrent menace to, or extinction of, other species. Both the growth in population and the loss of species can no longer be tolerated by the biosphere that sustains us – and thus rapid and drastic action is required.

As we constitute one of the components of this biosphere, its collapse would also mean the end of our own existence.

Early Phase and the Neolithic Revolution

Let us first take a closer look at the dramatic development of the Earth's human population. Its latest and most critical phase is illustrated in Fig. 1. Population figures during earlier phases are difficult to estimate with any accuracy. In any case, they were low in comparison to those during man's adoption of a new lifestyle at the beginning of the Neolithic Period. Indeed, by today's standards there were very few people living on the Earth. During the Neolithic Period, however, they began to practice agriculture and raise livestock. They began to settle down and thus laid the foundation for a completely new type of population structure and development.

Up to this point our ancestors had been hunters and gatherers and thus required relatively large areas for small groups of people. But general living conditions were so difficult that nearly all of the human-like primates that had emerged during the past several million years died out over the course of time. In the end only one line of development remained that finally led to today's human beings, *Homo sapiens*. Humans spent the great majority of their historical development as members of wandering and foraging groups. The crucial developmental phase from prehistoric man to sedentary farmer in the so-called hominization process lasted several million years.

The long and traditional way of life of hunters and gatherers changed for good as a result of revolutionary innovations during the Neolithic Period between 5000 and 10,000 years ago. However, these changes did not occur suddenly or take place everywhere at the same time. Different and often varying environmental conditions meant that for a long period of time the old and the new ways of living existed in different cultural circles concurrently, often side by side. Especially in the early phases they continued to be mixed to a large extent – if only for the reason that the difficult beginnings of farming and raising livestock did not make a sedentary lifestyle and the production of bread, vegetables, milk, cheese and meat substantially easier than wandering about in search of wild animals, fruit, roots and honey.

Even today the curse with which Adam and Eve were expelled from paradise is a bitter truth for many who have to feed themselves while farming barren land: "Cursed is the ground for thy sake; in sorrow shalt thou eat of it all the days of thy life." Only a minority of the inhabitants of the prosperous northern hemisphere know this firsthand. Most of them live in large cities and purchase food in an industrially processed form, often traveling from distant manufacturers in cans, bottles and plastic containers.

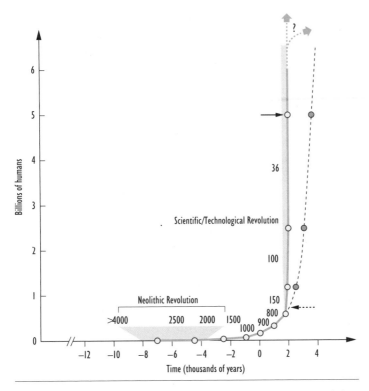

Figure 1 Leaps in human population growth as a result of the Neolithic and Scientific/Technological Revolutions (shaded areas)

The figures between open circles indicate the respective doubling times. The dashed line represents the hypothetical growth curve without the Scientific/Technological revolution: today's population level would not have been reached for another 1500 years; the dashed arrow indicates where it would be now. The solid arrow marks the end of the "Green Revolution," a short phase of unusual increases in agricultural productivity in numerous developing countries (p. 206)

The characteristic features of today's way of life – dense habitation, automated technology, industries organized as internationally operating concerns, global trade and transportation – would not be imaginable without this sedentariness that began with the domestication of plants and animals. Thus many historians have appropriately described this radical upheaval in human cultural history as the "Neolithic Revolution."

Fig. 1 illustrates the rate of human population growth, which was initially slow and then steadily increased for several millennia, until it exploded over the course of the last 200 to 300 years. Famines, epidemics and other natural catastrophes as well as wars have repeatedly led to regionally limited or even worldwide interruptions in this development. However, they are barely discernable in the curve's path which has risen so precipitously within no more than a few centuries.

The Scientific/Technological Revolution

Significantly, the curve is largely shaped by two great jumps. The first jump follows the Neolithic Revolution, which literally prepared the ground for the increasingly rapid doubling of the world's population. The second jump is marked by an even more dramatic change in the doubling time around the beginning of the 18th century, with the shortest doubling period of only 36 years occurring during the second half of the 20th century.

The dashed curve in Fig. 1 illustrates just what a dramatic change this second jump caused. This curve hypothetically assumes that the doubling time of the human population would have continued to shorten at the same rate as observed until the 17th century. In this case, the Earth would have had less than one billion inhabitants now, instead of the nearly seven billion we have today. It would have taken another 1500 years to reach the present mark. How much time we would have had together with subsequent generations in order to find solutions to all of the problems that now, within our lifetime, demand a fundamentally new type of global thought and action!

This most recent phase of human development in which the actual population explosion took place will be referred to as the Scientific/Technological Revolution. Together with the agrarian Neolithic Revolution, this second – still on-going – revolution – has had the greatest impact on the entire history of human cultural evolution. These two revolutions were incomparably more significant than the countless failed or successful coup attempts in the sense of a socio-political revolution. Although at first barely perceptible, they were long-term, radical, globally effective and irreversible upheavals that affected the entire sphere of human life. They were based neither on a political program – such as the French or Bolshevik Revolutions – nor on a specific invention, such as the light bulb or airplane. On the contrary, they were based on indirect and unintentional discoveries of fundamentally new possibilities, for example high-density urban life on the basis of large-scale, increasingly high-tech agriculture, or a high average life expectancy due to improved medical care on the basis of biological research and technology.

The Scientific/Technological Revolution of our epoch is such a complex event and has been of such vital importance to the subject of this book that I will deal with its historical development and its internal connections with the Neolithic Revolution in more detail in the following chapter. At this point two aspects are important: it was the Scientific/Technological Revolution that provided for the recent population explosion in its entire magnitude. And it is still in full swing and will be indispensable when it comes to solving the very problems it has created.

This becomes evident by looking at the upper end of the population curve in Fig. 1. The current rate of population growth must be stopped as quickly as possible. But today no one can forecast with any certainty when, at which level, and under what attendant circumstances such growth might actually come to a complete stop, especially as it has shifted from the northern hemisphere to Africa, parts of Asia and South America. It is therefore no longer within our sphere of direct influence. One of the most immediate problems is hence uncertain: the further development of the demand for food.

Reduced Biodiversity

If the agricultural use of the Earth's surface has not yet reached the breaking point for the remainder of the biosphere, then we can be certain that it soon will. And we do not have any appreciable reserves due to our current policy of surplus production in some particularly fertile areas. Despite its absolute level, this surplus is not very great in relative terms and could be used up very quickly if a crop failure occurs, for example, during a drought or exceedingly cold and wet period.

Our present dilemma becomes especially clear at this point. On the one hand, most pollsters predict rapid and unremitting growth in the world's population; unfortunately, however, without mentioning where the additional food, water, energy and living space should come from. On the other hand, we are already significantly contributing to a potential ecological catastrophe through the present excessive use of farmland and pastureland.

In this regard we are particularly effective. We maintain a few domesticated species, usually as monocultures, in huge fields

Figure 3   Wheat field as an example of the replacement of natural
biodiversity through intensive agriculture

which were once covered with highly diverse types of vegetation, e.g. forests, scrubland or savannas, thus removing invalu-
able evolutionarily adapted ecosystems. Current satellite pictures
and aerial photographs illustrate this situation with impressive
clarity (Fig. 2, color image I).

Such unnatural monocultures only thrive as a result of massive
human intervention (Fig. 3). They require the permanent use of
fertilizers and pesticides (and in the case of animals, concentrated feed and antibiotics) and are thus an additional existential
threat to the rest of the biosphere. Dwindling and polluted water
resources, encroaching deserts and toxic salt deposits on previously fertile land count among the increasingly serious results.

Will we be able to solve this dilemma at all? We must at least make every conceivable attempt to do so. Considering the magnitude and complexity of the problem, the initial attempt should be to divide it into manageable component parts. In order to prepare for this I will first list several premises, some of which I will comment upon in more detail at a later point:

- *Resignation is not a solution*
  Resignation means submitting to the seemingly inevitable; whoever is resigned to his fate cannot prevent anything from happening. It is understandable if an individual feels powerless in view of the advanced situation, the complexity of the causes and the global dimensions of species loss, air, soil and water pollution, as well as the ruthlessness with which natural resources are plundered and wasted.

  Each individual has only a very limited sphere of influence. But isn't the sum of these spheres of influence precisely the common public opinion with which individuals are able to exercise even more influence on important political decisions the more effectively they act within their own discrete spheres?

- *Science alone is powerless*
  Solving these imminent problems requires the cooperation of all active forces, ranging from the political, economic and scientific sectors to charity organizations and religious communities. Conversely, with regard to the subject of this book, science and technology alone can only offer possible solutions while leaving the actual implementation open. Scientific knowledge as such is of neutral value. Its *relative* value is

determined by the way we utilize it. The following statement is therefore even more relevant:

- *Responsibility increases along with scientific and technological progress*
  Progress literally implies putting one step in front of another. Turning this into a well-balanced process requires that roughly equal steps follow each other. In the latest era of human history we have made a great scientific and technological step forward. The present widespread uneasiness about the acceptance of further progress seems to indicate the impatience with which the compensating step – a responsible way of dealing with the results – is anticipated. There is no alternative to this second, corresponding step in the Scientific/Technological Revolution.

- *Cultural progress – including scientific research – is part of human evolution*
  We now find ourselves at a stage of unusually deep-rooted opposition to progress, which to some extent (see above) has occurred for very obvious reasons. One of these reasons may be a conscious or unconscious attempt at compensation for the widespread, uncritical belief in progress which prevailed in the 19th and the first half of the 20th centuries. However, progress is often mistaken for an advanced state and its continuation, and the fact that there is no alternative to progress is often overlooked. Progress is the inevitable result of a law of nature:

- *Evolution, be it cultural or biological, is an irreversible process*
  A time-dependent process, just as time itself, cannot run in

the reverse direction. There is no way to return to a previous state. Every state has its own parameters which change inexorably, and thus the initial position is irretrievably lost. "Back to nature" (as it once was) is not possible for the simple reason that every species in the process of natural evolution is constantly trying to adapt itself to its changing environment and therefore changes with it. Many are unsuccessful and become extinct – or wiped out. Correcting undesirable development like human overpopulation or other existential threats to the Earth's biosphere won't be possible by returning to a previous state. The only option we have is progress with new, qualitatively improved, and therefore contemporary means.

- *Advanced science is not omnipotent*
  The mystery of life has not been solved. A widespread misunderstanding assumes that scientific research has by now revealed every bit of essential knowledge and made it available for practical purposes. Unfortunately, pretentious scientists have been very effective in contributing to this misconception. Thus the erroneous impression has often been created that, after the spectacular findings in physics and chemistry at the beginning of the past century, biology has now unraveled the fundamentals of life and is about to replace creation – or more exactly and scientifically – the natural evolution of species with specifically targeted genetic modification.

  Within just a few decades, molecular biology has indeed provided a fascinating depth of insight into the miraculous world of life processes, including many details about inheritance and gene function. But just as elsewhere in science, more detailed knowledge in this area is a key to the more precise formulation of countless new, unanswered questions – especially with regard to the very basis of life.

In principle, there is most certainly agreement concerning these premises, even if they are modifiable to a certain extent. However, the prioritizing of our existential basic needs should be completely unquestionable:

> The highest priority for our very existence is a viable biosphere that provides us and everything else dependent upon it with a sufficient quality and quantity of the four basic elements of life: air, water, food and space to live.

Our situation is so threatened because two existential basic needs of equal standing – the preservation of a viable, human life supporting biosphere and the provision of all food from this source – work all the more against each other the more our population density increases:

- On the one hand, the *conservation of nature* is imperative on both a large and a small scale. Conservation does not primarily suggest being sentimental about beautiful and rare flowers and butterflies. It involves the conservation of our own species as well, i.e. self-protection. In practice this requires the conservation of individual specimens of threatened species as well as entire viable populations of as many species as possible: the greatest possible biodiversity. Conservation covers all parts of our biosphere: air, soil and water.
- However, in sharp contrast to this demand we are meeting our *nutritional needs* at the expense of the survival of increasing numbers of species. Providing a sufficient amount of food for several billion people is only possible through

the large-scale cultivation of high-yielding varieties of a
few different types of grains and other nutrient-rich and
productive field crops. These are grown annually around the
world in gigantic amounts, consumed and then discharged
as excrement. The demand for fertile parts of the Earth's
surface is accordingly great. These areas are no longer
available for their original natural biological diversity and
are therefore lost for nature conservation.

Agriculture is only one of many threats to our global biosphere.
Apart from clean air, potable water and space to live, food is our
most important basis of existence. We have no other choice but
to preserve the remainder of natural – or nearly natural – ecosystems through a qualitative improvement of agriculture. We can
limit, or even give up, every other economic sector in case of a
threat to our existence, however difficult. Agriculture is not up
for negotiation.

Practical Consequences

There are many options for ecologically beneficial improvements
based on available knowledge and opportunities. Wherever
economic and social relationships, as well as climate and soil
conditions permit, extensive ("nature-oriented") instead of cul-
ture-intensive forms of agriculture could be practiced. In places
such as mountainous regions, water protection areas or areas
with protected species we could largely forgo the intensive use of
synthetic fertilizers and chemical pesticides as well as large-scale
mechanized farming methods.

As necessary and beneficial contributions of this type may
be – especially in areas with unique and particularly threatened

biotopes – the growing worldwide demand for food cannot be satisfied without intensive agriculture.

For the purpose of effective nature conservation any escape from this dilemma demands that neither the intensively used agricultural parts of the Earth's surface be substantially expanded nor that destruction of the environment be allowed to continue on the present scale. Several courses of action are conceivable – in addition to every possible replacement of intensive with extensive agriculture – in order to find ecologically acceptable solutions to the problem. Every sensible contribution has to be considered here as well.

An especially obvious contribution is theoretically very simple and yet difficult to bring about in practical terms. It requires putting an end to all waste and distributing all the food produced worldwide in a need-based approach – as far as can be justified from a social, economic and environmental policy standpoint. Because it deals with the key question of our own behavior, I will limit myself here to this brief remark and deal with the subject at a later point (pp. 184ff.).

The immediate benefit from the sharing of surplus food would probably not even be very large in comparison with the total need. And yet, the importance of this kind of contribution, from an ecological as well as a psychological viewpoint, cannot be estimated highly enough.

A second course of action would probably not be any easier to pursue and also appears to be more simple in theoretical terms than in practice. It involves the production of considerably less meat in favor of the production of more food of direct plant origin and in favor of nature conservation. Where circumstances permit this would involve transforming areas used for animal feed production to areas for the cultivation of crops as a direct source of food for humans or, wherever it proves to make ecological sense, giving up grazing areas and forage crops in favor of increased nature conservation.

Since not every pasture can be turned into a productive field of crops and many pastures are in themselves biotopes worth protecting, the result could not be a complete abolition of animal farming. However, the benefit would be considerable in view of the simple calculation that every beefsteak has only 10% of the nutritional value of the feed used to produce it. In the case of chicken and pork the corresponding value is higher, but still only about 20%. I will comment on this in more detail at a later point (page 230).

The Challenge

If successful, all of the courses of action mentioned up to now would open up a certain number of additional food sources. However, the main problem would remain the conflict between the growing need for food and the unacceptability of further damage to the environment. Despite all other efforts, we still have to search for an effective way to drastically reduce the environmental impact of agriculture.

What would this course of action have to achieve in order for us to gain control over one of the greatest and most urgent problems of our time?

We have to remind ourselves once again that none of our most important agricultural crops could compete or survive in the wild without intensive human maintenance. Every one of them, developed over long periods of time as a high-yield crop plant, is dependent on intensive fertilization and sufficient protection against natural competitors (weeds) and enemies (especially insects and pathogens). Even under conditions of frequent crop rotation this requires the permanent use of large amounts of synthetic fertilizers, herbicides, insecticides, fungicides and other agrochemicals. Their use and production cause considerable amounts of air, soil and water pollution. The only answer is to look for and find fundamentally new methods of food production that take ecology into consideration.

We have every reason to regret this development with all of its varied consequences, but regret alone will not reverse it. Most of the more than six billion inhabitants depend on this type of high-yield agriculture, and in the very near future there will probably be many more. In this situation the almost utopian-sounding postulation is:

> We have to produce more high-quality food without
> substantially increasing the total area of farmland, while
> considerably reducing the overall environmental impact within
> the shortest possible time.

This is an immense, and yet crucially important challenge. And, among other measures (see Chapter 8), it essentially amounts to the accelerated breeding of new high-yield varieties of agricultural crops that require less fertilizers, pesticides and irrigation while still resulting in greater harvests.

In Chapter 4 we will see what a difficult obstacle the factor of time alone represents in plant breeding. Here is a comparison just for the sake of clarification: the Earth's population will have grown by another half a billion people in the five to ten years (a conservative estimate!) it takes to breed just one single modern cereal or potato variety. Even the best plant breeding program can't keep up with this pace – especially as long as it depends on multiple crossing and backcrossing generations – which usually involves a one-year generation time for each intermediate stage.

This limitation will in the long run be partially eliminated with genetic engineering, which involves the direct transfer of single carriers of hereditary information (genes), and will eventually allow for a greatly reduced breeding effort. It thus introduces a new dimension to plant breeding, but at the same time a new ethical dimension as well.

Within no more than ten years after the first commercial use of genetically modified plants in 1994 the area under cultivation in the eight most important producing countries (the United States, Argentina, Canada, Brazil, China, Paraguay, India and South Africa) had grown to 81 million hectares, nearly one-tenth of the total area of the USA or China. Altogether, there were approximately eight million farmers in seventeen countries cultivating genetically modified plants. And these figures are steadily increasing at high rates (from 81 million hectares in 2004 to 114 in 2007).

The challenge has thereby grown even larger. It consists of two parts of the same question. First of all, can genetic engineering be used in such a way that it benefits both existential basic needs, the provision of food *and* the conservation of nature? And secondly, what are the ethical boundaries of the practical use of genetic engineering? Fairly conclusive answers to both questions can only be found by looking at their historical background and at the status quo resulting from it.

I will therefore begin with a short overview of the historical development; there, where agriculture has its origins and where our present way of living began – in the New Stone Age, or Neolithic Period, about 10,000 years ago.

Summary

The alarming increase in the human population, with its immense need for agriculturally productive land and its growing environmental degradation, has pushed the Earth's biosphere to the breaking point. Qualitative progress must quickly lead to a type of agriculture that combines high productivity with a greatly reduced environmental impact and the sustainable protection of endangered species, water resources, soils and the climate. An analysis of the realistic possibilities thus concentrates on the questions of whether this aim is more easily attainable through the advancement of plant breeding with the aid of genetic engineering than without application of the latter and under what circumstances can the use of genetic engineering be justified.

2 Historical Development of Agriculture, Urban Lifestyles and Man's Perception of Nature

There are important reasons to consider the historical perspective when looking at upcoming developments in agriculture and plant breeding. We have to discover how we arrived at our present state of affairs and just how much freedom of choice we actually still have. How did our relationship to nature develop – especially with regard to agriculture and technology? What is the relationship between the new possibilities of plant genetic engineering and other scientific and technological developments? And which kinds of ethical questions do we have to consider and seek answers for?

Within the framework of this book such an overview can only be attained by making a few allusive jumps through the history of relevant cultural developments stretching back thousands of years. The usual professional subdivision of historical events may appear helpful at first view. Just as in the natural sciences and other branches of knowledge, the science of history divides its subject area into discernible segments (epochs). Although this simplifies the general overview, it often obscures the richness of smooth transitions.

The Greek philosopher Heraclitus' famous quote "everything is in a state of flux" not only expresses the unstoppable variableness of all things over time (his alternative poetic phrasing was "No one ever steps in the same river twice"), but also the vastly complex interaction of parallel events. Both aspects, the dynamism of succession and the interaction of simultaneous developments, need to be kept in mind when reflecting on particular historical events.

Early Stages of Cultural Evolution

The initial stages of evolution of today's *Homo sapiens* during the poorly defined hominization process are largely unknown. His novel and unique characteristic, specific to the development of humans, was his upright posture. This was a condition for the functional conversion of his ancestor's forefeet to hands, the enlargement of the skull and the brain, and the consequential anatomical and spiritual prerequisites for the development of intelligence, speech and technology. With their help, individually acquired information could be collected and passed on.

This biological and cultural evolution has been mutually beneficial since the beginning of the Stone Age, approximately two to five million years ago. For the first time in the Earth's history traditions were created which were no longer genetically anchored in the form of inherited instincts. Even approximately 500,000 years ago *Homo erectus* ("upright man") used fire and simple stone tools and handed these skills down to his descendents through new forms of communication. He had already become both *homo intellegens* and *homo technicus* – a being that thought, used self-made technological aids and continually "cultivated" both achievements.

The combined use of the brain and hands and their accelerated advancement were exceptional features unique to this species. They allowed Stone Age man to take a prominent position among all living creatures through a rapidly increasing – if unconscious – ability to influence his own evolution.

The genetic predisposition for the transformation of the hands and the enlargement of the brain as a prerequisite for the creation and passing on of cultural information was essentially existent. The key here was the use and strengthening of this potential through unconscious selection in accordance with new criteria. Favorable physical characteristics and advantageous instinctual behavior alone were no longer a measure of the ability to survive as intellectual aptitude became more and more important.

Positive feedback between these very diverse criteria increasingly accelerated the new process of evolution. Through intellectual and mechanical development humans began to acquire enormously expanded capacities to act and, if only relatively slowly and incompletely, to free themselves from an instinctual dominance. Just how strongly we nevertheless continue to be ruled by our overpowering instincts – despite all cultural progress – is most clearly shown by the continuous and unrestrained eruptions of aggression in its various emotionally, historically, religiously and socially motivated manifestations.

By the time the Mesolithic Period (Middle Stone Age) ended and the Neolithic Period (New Stone Age) began, humans had become the only higher life forms that had spread out into all inhabitable climate zones and continents. Even from this period they have left us numerous examples of their cultural achievements. And yet, this new result of biological evolution, the thinking human, whose intellect secured its survival and advancement, also contained an ambivalence: the freedom of choice and the knowledge of good and evil, which has inescapably accompanied human existence ever since.

Presumably due to this ambivalence, ethical values were formed early and, together with technological achievements, became a major part of human culture.

Figure 4   Rock painting from the Middle Stone Age

Walking archer (Valtorta Gorge, Spain)

Among the admirable achievements of older Stone Age humans were their artistic manifestations. Countless remarkably expressive petroglyphs, in Europe mainly preserved as cave paintings from the last ice age period (approximately 30,000 to 10,000 BC), provide us with insight into the imagination and living conditions of people who felt completely at the mercy of overwhelming nature: the magical evocation of hunting success, demons, fertility and courage in battle. Fig. 4 shows a typical example.

Small and isolated groups of hunters and gatherers suffered the omnipresent threats of hunger, illness, wild animal attack and other natural forces. The world appeared full of sinister and adverse powers. All of the other lines of evolution, which began as prehistoric man, had become extinct long before.

It is obvious to assume that man, in the beginning of conflicting priorities between the mental feeling of helplessness and the intellectual and technical ability of action and expression, was able to draw hope from three very different sources: from the ability to communicate and express empathy; from the belief in the effect of magic arts; and through rapid technological progress along the path he had chosen to follow.

In addition to artistic renderings, the technological achievements of older prehistoric man have been proven through many archaeological findings. An abundance of roughly worked hatchets, lances and arrowheads, scrapers and other Stone Age tools of various types were made at the same time the petroglyphs were created. They testify to a state of producing and using technology that now enabled people to enter a new era of cultural development. Stone Age man had reached a technical and intellectual level of development that opened up a completely new way of life through the growing of crops and animal husbandry.

The Fertile Crescent

This new developmental step was the beginning of the Neolithic Revolution. Although the actual revolutionary event – with all its long-term consequences – was the domestication of animals and plants, there were additional factors as well. Global climatic changes were especially drastic. They caused the end of the last great ice age and therefore the radical transformation of vegetation zones. Humans were forced to adapt either by migrating huge distances or by changing their way of life.

After the retreat of the ice, living conditions in Central and

Northern Europe changed particularly drastically. At first open tundra developed with numerous lakes of all sizes, and meat acquired through hunting and the catching of fish and birds became amply available. As the temperature increased birch, pine, and finally, mixed oak forests spread throughout the landscape, which in turn caused a corresponding change in the fauna. Game for hunting now consisted mainly of wild boar, roe deer, stag, bear, elk and wild ox instead of reindeer and bison. Instead of following herds of animals for long distances, people were able to spend more time in permanent settlements.

Although post-ice age warming affected the flora and fauna in different climate zones in diverse ways, thus affecting human living conditions as well, human cultural development independently reached similar levels around the world. The use of stone tools and fire had been Stone Age man's first great discoveries as *homo faber*, as a craftsman. Stone tools enabled the production of additional wooden and bone devices. Stone as a material was of such great importance to human cultural development that it gave its name to the first and longest of all epochs, the Stone Age.

A third great achievement on the way to the Neolithic Revolution – after the use of stone and fire – was the first new technological creation of human intelligence: the production of ceramics. For the first time in its history mankind created items through the specific reshaping of a naturally occurring raw material. Moist clay was shaped into the desired form from a malleable lump, "fired" in an oven and thus transformed into a rock-hard material. The result was a completely changed product that could be used for a new purpose, and – in contrast to all materials used before – could not be restored to its original state. Figurines made of fired clay have even been found in the encampments of Stone Age mammoth hunters in South Moravia (Dolni Vestonice, approximately 23,000 BC).

Figure 5   Venus of "Tepe Sarab"
            An idol of fertility made of
            fired clay, approximately 6000
            BC

The creative possibilities of producing fired clay figures must have greatly impressed people who lived during the Ceramic Age. In both of the major Near Eastern creation stories, the Epic of Gilgamesh and the Old Testament, Enkidu and Adam were respectively formed from loam or "clods of earth." Today we admire the creative power and the capacity for abstract thinking of the people who so expressively created ceramic figures such as the "Venus of Tepe Sarab" (see Fig. 5) approximately 8000 years ago.

The practical application of this new technology was the production of ceramic vessels. This did not occur everywhere at the same time as the domestication of plants and animals, but was another important precondition of a more sedentary lifestyle with the corresponding need to store food, another characteristic of the Neolithic Revolution.

The smooth transitions and diverse initial conditions make it very probable that the change from a nomadic-gathering to a sedentary-producing economy occurred independently in several instances; not only on different continents, but in geographically adjacent regions as well. The prototype of the fixed settlement was probably an encampment that was put to repeated use and

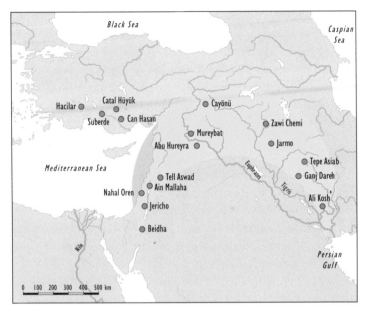

Figure 6   Fertile Crescent with archaeological excavation and finding
sites from the early Neolithic Revolution

eventually became a stationary base as people wandered less and
less, given a sufficient food supply and protection against adverse
weather and enemies.

The oldest archaeological findings of larger urban settlements are found in Asia Minor and in the Middle East in the
area of the Fertile Crescent (Fig. 6). Among the most famous
of these early cities are Jericho, Jarmo and Çatal Hüyük where,
using modern excavation and dating methods, it has been shown
that the building of houses, animal husbandry and agriculture
occurred as early as the seventh millennium before Christ. In
Çatal Hüyük for instance, the domestication of barley, einkorn,

emmer, wheat, peas, lentils and vetches as well as dogs, sheep and cattle had already taken place. Extensive trade with clam shells and obsidian was apparently quite common and knowledge of animal husbandry and the cultivation of plants as well as their products must have been widespread. Not all of the wild ancestors of the domesticated plants and animals could have originated from this area.

There is every indication that one of the first origins of the Neolithic Revolution was in the region of the Fertile Crescent, between the Mediterranean Sea and the foothills of the Himalayas. Numerous other independent centers of human settlement have now been discovered through archaeological research. An interesting example is the Tehuacán Valley in modern day Mexico, where domesticated pumpkin and pepper varieties dating from 7000 BC have been found.

Both centers, in Central America as well as in Asia Minor, are nevertheless at the same time impressive examples of early environmental catastrophes caused by humans. Many previously fertile and wooded regions in the eastern Mediterranean area have been robbed of their soil and become infertile as a result of large-scale deforestation and grazing. Similarly reckless agricultural overuse could have contributed to the demise of the once-blossoming Maya culture.

In addition to the remains of buildings, tools and utensils, and domesticated or collected plants and domesticated or hunted animals, excavations of early settlements have unearthed a plethora of cultural objects from the time of the Neolithic Revolution. Especially numerous are seated female figurines made of clay; a particularly revealing one is shown in Fig. 5. In unrivalled symbolic clarity, they emphasize the unity of fertility and an affinity with the Earth which became a conscious basis of life and survival for settled agrarian people. In the ritual adoration of such idols of fertility (as well as a well-established cult of death) they demonstrated an increased awareness of a dependence on natural cycles of growth and transitoriness as well as the success of their own – skilled and ritual – cultivation of food sources.

Advanced Civilizations of the Bronze Age

The next big breakthrough led from stone to metal as the basis of tools and utensils. Once again it was a very gradual transition, as the name "Chalcolithic Period" (Copper Age) implies for the period between the Neolithic and Bronze Age. This transition was again very smooth and variable with regard to both timing and location.

Probably the most convincing example of the simultaneous existence of different stages of tool usage are cultures in Africa, Australia and Oceania that still work with stone tools while most other cultures, after more or less distinctive Bronze and Iron Ages, use new metal alloys, silicon semiconductors and synthetic plastics with a rapidly increasing variety of characteristics.

In addition to the technological progress of metal processing, on an intellectual level the invention of script was one of the most important cultural achievements of people who had adopted a settled lifestyle. These were the same people who had already founded mighty city-states just a few millennia after Jericho, Jarmo and Çatal Hüyük. The oldest findings to date of image-like predecessors of a later cuneiform script come from the Sumerian Uruk (the biblical Erech, now called Warka) on the lower Euphrates. A cult vase of impressive artistic achievement with noteworthy motifs from the fourth millennium BC was found during excavations of the temple district of the fertility goddess Inanna (Ischtar) (Fig. 7).

Figure 7   Cult vase from Uruk (approximately 3500 BC) with early evidence of a sedentary lifestyle, as described in the accompanying text

Figure 8   Sculpture of a woman's
head ("Goddess" or
"Lady") from Uruk,
approximately 3200 BC

This alabaster cult vase illustrates the basis of existence at that time in an artistically condensed form: water, agriculture, livestock farming and ritual activities. At the bottom, undulating lines symbolize water as the basic necessity for growing cultivated plants (ears of grain and young date palms), which then serve as feed for the domesticated animals (sheep). Both of these serve as food for humans, who are carrying some of this fare in front of them as offerings in the middle frieze. At the top a priest brings the offerings to a divine being, presumably Inanna, the goddess of fertility, love and war, who is recognizable due to her characteristic bundles of reeds (fertility and waging war for fertile areas were probably intrinsic parts of life from the beginning and were therefore ritually worshipped together).

At the same excavation site an impressive, slightly more recent alabaster sculpture of a woman's head was found (Fig. 8) which, in comparison to Fig. 5, attests to the large leap in cultural development during this early phase of urban life.

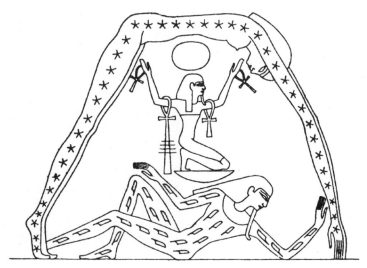

Figure 9   Ancient Egyptian depiction of the sky goddess Nut above Geb,
            the god of the earth

Together they form a passageway for the sun on its way around the earth.
Kneeling between them is Shu, the god of the air and light

Priesthood, especially in connection with the fertility cult,
obviously played a dominant role in the social structure at that
time. Other than temples and houses, no palaces of secular
rulers were found at excavation sites. A heavenly father (temporarily a divine king as well) gradually took over the dominant
position that the mother goddess (earth mother) had occupied
until then. Many gods in the epochs to follow were part human,
part animal, sun, or moon.

The diminishing superiority of a fertile Mother Nature, or
Mother Earth, testifies to the transition from the magical to the
mystical perception of nature. The Egyptian depiction of the
firmament in Fig. 9 is a notable example of the inclusion of the

supernatural into what had been a mindscape characterized by earthly fertility, and earthly gods and demons.

Especially favorable conditions for a settled life organized in an urban manner were found in fertile alluvial plains in the climatically moderate zones of the land between the Euphrates and Tigris Rivers (Mesopotamia), the Middle and Lower Nile, as well as similar large river valleys in India, China, and other parts of the world. On the Euphrates, Tigris and Nile the first large empires of the Sumerians and Egyptians flourished, and later those of the Assyrians and Babylonians, whose early cultural prosperity greatly influenced Europe's development after spreading through Crete, Greece, and Rome. The early precursors of modern science were created with writing and the first depictions of abstract concepts (e.g. a clay vessel for "design"), the discovery of systems of numbers, units of measure and a calendar, as well as astronomy and astrology.

The development of a new lifestyle with a division of labor in villages and urban areas as well as the concentration on especially fertile areas resulted in strong population growth during the first few thousand years of settled life – rough estimates suggest an increase from approximately 10 to 20 million around 7000 BC to almost 100 million by 4000 BC. The gradual transition of state power from the temple priests to secular rulers led to a greater differentiation in the social structure. The economic basis of agriculture and animal husbandry provided for the increasingly rapid development of religion, arts and science, bureaucracy, technology, architecture, trade and shipping, but at the same time led to an intensification of war and slavery.

Agricultural technology developed rapidly. People used plows and draft animals, built artificial irrigation systems and granaries, baked bread in ovens, brewed beer and, after setting fixed values, traded goods while using cereal grains, other natural products, jewelry, copper, and silver as means of payment.

Even catastrophic floods, including the "Great Flood," which according to nearly identical reports in the Epic of Gilgamesh and the Bible had devastating results (excavations have now uncovered a layer of mud of several meters in thickness from approximately 4000 BC), were unable to impede the change to a more settled lifestyle and the resultant population increase for long. A new type of differentiated human cultural development began here, as in many other regions of the Earth around that time. This was made possible and furthered by a productive form of agriculture, the steady expansion of which was programmed from now on and could no longer be reversed. Several of the most fertile river valleys and plains in Europe, North Africa, the Middle East, India, China, and Central and South America became early human cultural landscapes as a result of the Neo-lithic Revolution.

European Antiquity in Greece and Rome

During the peak of early advanced civilizations in the Bronze Age a rational way of thinking gradually began to overlay the transition from a magical to a mythical view of the world. This was especially obvious in the remarkable knowledge that the early Sumerian, Babylonian, Egyptian, Indian, Chinese, and New World civilizations acquired through systematic observation of the heavens and utilization of these observations in mathematics and in the invention of calendar systems. This knowledge finally led to the beginnings of scientific astronomy in the 6th century BC as the Babylonians began to predict the movements of the sun, moon, and the planets as well as the occurrence of eclipses. This new type of astronomy, which for the first time was scientifically verifiable through predictions, was nevertheless still firmly connected to the astrology and mythology from which it had arisen.

The first great western mathematicians and natural philosophers (Thales and Anaximander of Miletus, Pythagoras of Samos, and Heraclitus of Ephesus) initiated the next great breakthrough in self-examination and the observation of nature in the 6th century BC. A new form of independent and rational thinking began, based on astronomy and mathematics in the Sumerian, Babylonian, and Egyptian traditions, which had a significant influence on agricultural practices as well.

At that time the Earth was considered to be a disc with a contiguous mainland surrounded by the ocean like an island. It is not hard to imagine how Thales, while carrying out calculations on this disc, came up with his famous theorem about a right triangle over the diameter of a circle. A short time later Pythagoras advocated an astronomical view of the world in which the Earth, now portrayed as a globe, circled around a "central fire" in an integral spherical harmony together with the sun, the moon, the planets and the fixed stars. And Heraclitus described this world as being in a state of constant change and renewal, controlled by inherent reason (*logos*). Consequently, the world should only be comprehensible through logical thinking.

The big breakthrough consisted in the completely new referencing of this conception of the world to humans as thinking subjects and individuals. "Man is the measure of all things," the sophist Protagoras exclaimed. And thus the ground was prepared for the three preeminent philosophers Socrates, Plato, and Aristotle, who as a direct continuum of teacher and pupil together created a body of thought toward the end of the 5th and 4th centuries BC that has lost little of its influence and lasting power up to the present.

Through critical questioning and a rational comparison of arguments Socrates attempted to reach an unprejudiced, philosophical-scientific way of thinking and independent moral integrity. In the "Forms" his pupil Plato saw the archetype of mundane objects, the mathematical regularity and harmony of which allowed humans to recognize the world. In the end, his pupil Aristotle summarized the knowledge of this epoch in an independent work which was unique in its scope and complexity and which was, for the first time, based on the formal distinction of scientific disciplines.

Aristotle's work represented the actual beginning of intellectually independent, experimental science, even if several pre-Socratic philosophers and others after them, especially Leucippus and Democritus, had already developed some of the natural scientific body of thought through their theories about the atomic composition of matter.

Once again the visual arts provided a sensitive measure of the ongoing transition from the magical and the mythical to a rational view of the world and its new center – human beings themselves. Vase paintings, frescos, reliefs, and sculptures designed in a naturalistic and, at the same time, humanly expressive style were created at the time of the three great philosophers and had a crucial influence on art in the Hellenic and Roman empires founded by Aristotle's pupil Alexander the Great. A classical Greek example of this next large leap forward is shown in Fig. 10, in contrast to the illustrations of earlier times in Figs. 5 and 8.

This new jump in human cultural and developmental history was made possible by the then firmly established urban lifestyles of history's most influential civilizations. Many city-states and empires fought bitterly with each other over fertile agricultural areas and for political and economic supremacy, which they perpetually won and lost.

Figure 10   Classical Greek depiction of the goddess Athena Lemnia

Roman copy of a marble statue made by the Greek sculptor Pheidias in approximately 440 BC

The establishment (or conquest) of an efficient agricultural system, often including distant migrations, had long since become an indispensable prerequisite for political, economic, and cultural success. Domesticated crops and farm animals were thus transported further and further from the areas where they originated, and the technical means of irrigating, controlling floods, working the soil, harvesting, as well as storing and transporting seed and food became more sophisticated.

Of the many written reports about the agriculture of antiquity, the didactic poem the *Georgics* written by the Roman poet Virgil (70 to 19 BC) is the most comprehensive and well-known. In four volumes he wrote detailed and vivid descriptions about cultivating the land, tree care, animal husbandry, and beekeeping. The following short excerpt from a longer treatise about crop rotation and fertilization gives us an idea of knowledge at the time:

"Then thou shalt suffer in alternate years
The new-reaped fields to rest, and on the plain
A crust of sloth to harden; or, when stars
Are changed in heaven, there sow the golden grain
Where erst, luxuriant with its quivering pod,
Pulse, or the slender vetch-crop, thou hast cleared,
And lupin sour, whose brittle stalks arise,
A hurtling forest. For the plain is parched
By flax-crop, parched by oats, by poppies parched
In Lethe-slumber drenched. Nathless by change
The travailing earth is lightened, but stint not
With refuse rich to soak the thirsty soil,
And shower foul ashes o'er the exhausted fields.
Thus by rotation like repose is gained,
Nor earth meanwhile uneared and thankless left.
Oft, too, 'twill boot to fire the naked fields,
And the light stubble burn with crackling flames"

At the time the *Georgics* was written (approximately 30 BC) there were already four million Roman citizens, and fertile Egypt had been turned into the breadbasket of a growing world empire to secure their supply of food. The new Roman province of Gaul already had between six and seven million inhabitants and the world's total population had grown to more than 150 million by this time. Although the Roman Empire had not yet reached its zenith the beginnings of internal decay became apparent through the luxury of the upper class, increasing urbanization (including the free distribution of food to the poor), and the dissolution of free peasantry.

From the Middle Ages to the Modern Era

With the ending of the Roman Empire the center of political and economic power increasingly shifted from southern to southwestern and then to western and central Europe. No other epoch is as difficult to define as the "Middle Ages" (also referred to as the medieval period) when this shift took place. It is the time period between Antiquity and the Modern Era, approximately between AD 500 and 1500 (to some historians it began between AD 800 and 1000). The structure of the settled lifestyle had become so permanent by the time the Middle Ages began that society could be roughly divided into three classical groups: the food producing working-class (farmers), the military profession (knights), and the teaching profession (clergy).

The high level of agricultural development in ancient Rome had changed little by the early and high Middle Ages. The world's population grew steadily until the beginning of the plague pandemics in the 14th century. During the late Middle Ages this caused the increased villagization of what had previously been widely scattered farming communities, primarily in Central Europe, as well as a migration from the countryside to cities and the development of new settlement areas in the eastern parts of Europe.

Today there are still groups of ethnic Germans in Eastern Europe that provide evidence of these medieval emigrations. The legend of The Pied Piper of Hamelin is known around the world, but not many people know that the historic essence of the story is about the city's young adults who were wooed away (the "exodus of the children" in 1284) to settle regions further to the east. Increasing population pressure, political and economic interests, and a general deterioration of the climate in 13th century Europe may have been the main causes for this kind of collective migration.

Even in densely populated areas agriculture was expanded through intensive deforestation, the draining of swamps and marshes or the construction of dikes near the ocean and river mouths. Europe ultimately became a human cultural landscape. There were also new developments in agricultural practice with the introduction of crop rotation (e.g. three different crops in annual turns), the turning plow, and the harrow. Due to increasing urbanization a new agricultural commodities market and a growing monetary economy were created. All this contributed substantially to the gradual emancipation of farmers from a long period of serfdom in the feudalistic system of the Middle Ages.

The devastating plague pandemics were among the most profound events of the late Middle Ages. Together with other epidemics they resulted in the death of approximately 25 million people in Europe between 1348 and 1350, almost a third of the population at that time. An extensive abandonment of villages and land followed, and agriculture recovered very slowly. Among other consequences, the abandonments led to an intensification of animal husbandry and to a temporary ample supply of meat, even in large cities. Thousands of oxen, many from eastern European areas, were driven into these cities each year.

The recurring deadly pandemics and epidemics of plague, leprosy, typhoid fever, and cholera, as well as failed harvests and other "judgments of God" were certainly one of the reasons for the deep and often mystical devoutness of the people during the Middle Ages. No other epoch has produced religiously motivated works of art in such an abundance, intensity, or artistic

Figure 11   Madonna by Tilman Riemenschneider (about 1510)

perfection, ranging from the large cathedrals with their sculptures, glass windows, and altarpieces to miniature paintings in Evangeliaria and other texts. An impressive example of religious internalization, in comparison to Fig. 10, is depicted in the wooden sculpture of a late medieval Madonna in Fig. 11.

The flipside of this piety were the murderous crusades, robber barons, a merciless inquisition, superstition, religious mass hysteria, and apprehension about the end of the world. Only by looking at this great contradiction is it possible to understand just how painstaking the process of rebirth (Renaissance) of the ancient world view was with the development of our current rational sciences. All the more, the beginning of the Modern Era was a slow but powerful revolution which affected all aspects of life, comparable in its sweeping effect only to the dramatic upheavals of the Neolithic Revolution.

Once again it wasn't a single key event which marked the beginning of the Modern Era. Several complementary developments came together more or less by chance, particularly during the decisive period of mental transition to rational approaches from the middle of the 15th century to the beginning of the 16th century. After the fall of Constantinople (1453) and the retaking of Granada (1492) the world's power was concentrated more than ever before in the west, in the center, and soon also in the north of Europe. These new centers of power were able to acquire a large share of the cultural treasures of southeastern Europe and the Orient, especially from Constantinople. At the same time, Christopher Columbus, Vasco da Gama, Ferdinand Magellan and other seafarers discovered previously unknown continents and conquered them as colonies of the Western European kingdoms.

As secular power increased the disentanglement of art and science from the dominating influence of the church progressed rapidly. Painting discovered the rationally perceived spatial perspective and the landscape as a natural background in pictures. Equally rational and object-related became the approaches of those branches of science that freed themselves in reminiscence of Aristotle and his forerunners as "natural scientists" from the thousand-year-old unity with Christian theology and philosophy. While seafarers demonstratively proved the Earth was round, Nicolas Copernicus founded a new heliocentric world view that was refined over the next two centuries by Johannes Kepler, Galileo Galilei, and Isaac Newton into one of the foundations of today's physical science. Paracelsus, a contemporary of Copernicus, advocated the self-help of nature in empirical medicine supported by pharmaceutical chemistry.

Figure 12   Medieval map of the world from the 11th century

"T and O maps" were not drawn to scale and showed Asia at the top, Europe at the bottom left, and Africa at the bottom right. The continents were divided by the T-shaped Mediterranean Sea and surrounded by the encircling Ocean

All of this spread quickly as a result of the introduction of new techniques for typography and the manufacturing of paper from linen. Half a century after the invention of letterpress printing with movable type (by Johannes Gutenberg around 1450) over 1000 printers throughout Europe had already produced approximately ten million pieces of printed matter.

The great contrast between the old and the new view of the world is illustrated in Figs. 12 and 13. Up to the end of the Middle Ages the Earth was often depicted on a stylized "T and O map" as a disc divided into three sections showing those parts of the Earth that were then known (Asia, Europe and Africa). Exact contours or relative sizes played no role with regard to these maps (Fig. 12).

In contrast to this traditional view, the woodcut entitled *Man Breaks through the Firmament and Recognizes the Spheres* illustrates the dramatic transformation of the world's physical perception (Fig. 13). Especially remarkable is the complete demythologizing of the firmament, which in contrast to Fig. 9, is depicted as obeying rational mechanical laws.

This rational approach took hold of all areas of the natural

Figure 13 Woodcut by Claude Flammarion (late 19th century)
illustrating the mechanical image of the world after the
"Copernican Revolution"
See text for further explanation

sciences and medicine. Today, about 500 years after the revival
of a purely empirical, inductive, and evidence-oriented type of
science, it is hard to imagine that at the end of the Middle Ages
numerical data and graphic representations of people, animals,
plants, stars, and other objects still had a predominantly religious symbolic character. Toward the end of the 15th century
these objects were finally given their own identities and thus had
anatomical instead of symbolic qualities. Leonardo da Vinci
depicted humans and plants as anatomical objects of study and

consequently became known as the founder of scientific illustration. The artist himself was given a new personal identity as he began to sign his works of art.

At the same point in time seafarers brought unknown plants, animals, and people to Europe from distant parts of the Earth, predominantly as curious showpieces that were exhibited at fairs or in cloister and palace gardens. Conversely, everything in Europe that could be transported and did not already exist elsewhere was exported to the newly discovered continents, especially countless crops and farm animals along with the conquerors and colonists that expelled or subdued the indigenous peoples and claimed the land for their Crown. Inevitably, numerous human, animal, and plant pathogens were spread far and wide by their carriers, with the tragic consequences that many American Indian tribes were largely eradicated by foreign diseases, and plant and animal pests and diseases were distributed throughout the world.

Despite the rapid conquest and settlement of large colonial areas by European maritime powers, the largest part of the Earth's surface was still unknown to the Western world at this time. In AD 1400 Europeans knew only about 20% of the Earth's surface. Even by 1600, after 100 years of colonization, this figure had increased to no more than 40%, and by 1900 to 90%.

To the expanding human population in the 15th and 16th centuries the natural environment probably still appeared to be inexhaustible, indestructible and overwhelmingly rich in diversity and resilience.

The Present

Today, at the beginning of the 21st century, we are experiencing the increasingly rapid tempo of development of rational thought, which had been definitively demythologized at the beginning of the Modern Era and thus initiated an uncontested Scientific/ Technological Revolution. Less than 500 years after wind-pow-ered sailing ships conquered continents previously unknown to Europe, and after the successive invention of steamships, gaso-line engines, propeller-driven airplanes and jet engines, manned missions to the moon and the detailed exploration of nearly all the planets with ingeniously equipped space probes have become commonplace.

Every square meter of our own planet is either known to us or easy to reach at any time through the use of existing means. Airplanes and helicopters now take us everywhere on the planet within a very short amount of time, while less than two centuries ago Alexander von Humboldt, David Livingstone, and count-less others explored barely accessible areas, often never seen by Europeans before, in extremely dangerous and difficult voyages of discovery. Today all the blank spots that our grandparents or great grandparents used to look at in their school atlases have disappeared.

Investigations of the natural world that surrounds us, the macrocosm as well as the microcosm, is making spectacular progress. Only 500 years after the seemingly flat earth finally became accepted as a globe and was no longer seen as the center of the universe, Albert Einstein's theory of relativity and the discovery of molecular genetics have once again revolutionized our view of the world. The great line that connects these revo-lutionary breakthroughs is clearly recognizable. It begins with the Babylonian, Egyptian and Greek astronomers and natural philosophers, leads to Copernicus, Galileo, Newton, and Einstein, and on to space travel. In biology and medicine, it has led by way of Paracelsus and many others to today's medical research and pharmacotherapy, which have risen to an unimaginable level as a result of molecular biology and genetic engineering.

Recognizing our own nature, despite depth psychology, neuroscience and social science, has proven to be a nearly impossible undertaking, even though this is the only means of coping with the numerous problems that we have now brought upon ourselves. Recognizing, understanding, and mastering many impulsive behavior patterns that were once necessary for survival, especially individual and collective aggression and self-indulgence, is now one of the most urgent tasks facing us.

We have extended our five senses through the invention of all kinds of highly sensitive measuring devices in order to precisely determine the composition of distant stars or our own genes. These devices are constructed and used by experts who, with increasing specialization, know more and more about their own fields of expertise and less and less about all others. The common "bosom of the church" experienced during medieval times, which despite all its contradictions gave western Christendom a feeling of unity and individual security, has receded into the distance for a majority of people at the beginning of the 21st century.

The loss of the Earth, and thus of humankind, as the physical and psychological center of the universe has two complementary effects that shape our current era more than anything else. On the one hand, humans have changed from the self-experienced role of subjects determined by external forces (while still occupying center stage) to that of active scientific conquerors and technological dominators who, on the other hand, have lost their religious orientation and now feel the new burden of individualization, forlornness and the search for a deeper meaning.

Figure 14 Edvard Munch, "The Scream" (1895)

Once again the visual arts express this change from religious integration to isolation and forlornness in a particularly expressive manner. Many modern works of art cry out for a new conjoining center, even if this is seldom direct (Fig. 14), but rather in abstract forms as a stylized torso, a luminous stimulus, a deafening metal construction, or as a silent sheaf of searching lines (Fig. 15). As such, they are much more cryptic and difficult to decipher than a medieval altarpiece.

The simultaneous path that philosophy took into nihilism and existentialism in search of a new self-image received its first harsh manifestation in Friedrich Nietzsche's *Thus Spoke Zarathustra*, "Once blasphemy against God was the greatest blasphemy; but God died, and therewith also those blasphemers. To blaspheme the earth is now the dreadfulest sin, and to rate the heart of the unknowable higher than the meaning of the earth!" Such statements represented the sensitive flipside of individual emancipation and the concurrent explosive increase and spread

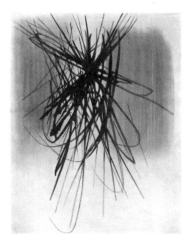

Figure 15 Hans Hartung,
"T-1958–2" (1958)

of the human population, especially in and from Europe, over
the entire Earth as well as the equally explosive increase in scientific knowledge and technological achievements.

Despite two world wars the Earth's population managed to
double itself for the first time in no more than 100 years between
1850 and 1950. As compensation for shortages and yield fluctua-
tions grain and chilled meat had long since become important
economic factors not just within Europe, but around the world,
especially in the areas with large surpluses like North America,
Argentina, Australia, and New Zealand. At the beginning of the
20th century Russia and India were still among the most important wheat exporting countries.

The last time a large proportion of the European population had little to eat was during the period immediately following World War II. In many of the war-stricken countries
the supply of food, especially towards the end of the war and
in the first post-war years was on average considerably below

the subsistence level. At the same time, after years of producing armaments and enduring destruction, many countries were also short on the most important consumer goods. The two primary goals of post-war economies were thus the full-scale production of foodstuffs and material commodities.

Hardly anyone, least of all those in the agricultural sector, foresaw either the speed with which the economies of western industrial countries and Japan would reach the intended goal of market saturation or the boundlessness of the consumer goods industry (once set in motion) as it went from *satisfying actual demand* to influencing and promoting the *creation of demand*. Today kiwi fruit and apples from New Zealand, beef from Argentina, wine from South Africa, Australia, Chile, and California, fruit and vegetables on a year-round basis from the southern Mediterranean area, and many other foodstuffs and luxuries from all over the world are extolled on a European market that spends vast sums for the production, storage, and destruction of its own goods.

This surplus is produced at the expense of the environment and social well-being and thus is no longer tenable. Apart from this environmental and social concern, it is too insignificant and too dearly bought to solve food shortage problems in other parts of the world. The hunger that Europe experienced after the two world wars and especially after failed harvests in the 19th century, which led to large waves of emigration (particularly to North and South America), is now concentrated in the "third world" of former colonies in Africa, Asia, and Latin America.

Agriculture in industrialized countries has reached a high standard of production thanks to the development of science and technology, while at the same time rapidly reducing the number of those employed in this sector. Two hundred years ago the ratio of those working in agriculture to the rest of the population was

4:1; today in many industrialized countries this figure is close to 1:50. Two of the most serious social consequences are large-scale unemployment and the continuous exodus of the rural population to large cities. Many urban centers already have more than ten million inhabitants, equal to the total population of the Earth at the beginning of the Neolithic Revolution. By comparison, Cologne, the largest Central European city during and for some time after the Middle Ages, had approximately 35,000 inhabitants at the end of the 16th century. Few cities in Western and Southern Europe had more than 100,000 residents at this time.

The social problems that have resulted from individual isolation, the population explosion, increasing automation, and the unequal distribution of prosperity, employment, education, health care and food are presumably more difficult to overcome than anything else that we are now confronted with. On the other hand, the natural limits which our environment sets to our population pressure are the least flexible and therefore present us with a challenge that is at least as great, especially for agriculture.

Summary

Three major developmental steps were crucial for the rapid cultural evolution of humans: upright posture (including all the subsequent anatomical consequences right up to intelligence and language), a settled life as a result of agriculture and animal husbandry, and the extension of the range of action through science and technology. The transformation from appropriation to the production of food fostered new forms of settlement and the creation of sophisticated social structures with a broad division of labor. This change in lifestyle enabled a growing emphasis on science and technology; in the biological sector all the way from the early stages of food production to molecular biology and genetic engineering.

With the extension of consciousness and knowledge, humans advanced – in terms of self-assessment – from passive subjects that experienced nature as a dominating power to active individuals that attempted to gain control over all parts of their environment. And yet, every cultural and technological progression was a step in the increasingly dangerous direction of dependence on a threatened biosphere. Thus progress became synonymous with an obligation to constantly improve those agricultural achievements without which this evolution would not have taken place.

3 Man and His Environment

The sudden turnabout from the discovery and appropriation of our environment to the increasing threat to it has clearly shown us our limits when it comes to growth. Such limits manifest themselves not only through the density of our population and production of food, but just as much through our production of "luxury goods" and the consequences of this extravagance.

If we are not willing to risk our very existence, then we have to be more considerate of our environment and take the necessary precautions in order to preserve it over the long term. With this in mind it would be helpful to take another look at our evolution from a different perspective.

The First Two Phases: Founding and Securing Human Existence

From the point of view of its own evolution, *Homo sapiens* has completed two formative phases of development and is now at a critical stage of a third phase. In the first phase, which ended with the Neolithic Revolution, a new form of biological existence was founded through the preferred development of the brain and the hands, i.e. intelligence and technology. One of the characteristics of evolution is the fact that this successfully initiated development not only continued during the second phase, which was concerned with securing this existence, but even continuously increased as a result of positive feedback.

It now appears that this second phase of securing our existence to the greatest extent possible has also been completed; however, not the cultural evolution of humans. Neither intelligence nor technology have reached any clear goals. Will an even greater emphasis on intelligence and technology be the most important characteristic of the current third phase of our evolution? Will solidarity and precaution replace the appropriation and exploitation of nature?

An inability to answer these questions does not make them pointless. They help us to extrapolate between the past and the future and to thus draw conclusions. And this could put us in a position to positively influence the course taken by the third phase.

Natural evolution, the interplay of emergence and extinction as well as the advancement and retreat of individual species, is a dynamic process that extends over long periods of time – on average substantially longer than our own species has existed. Two characteristics, however, distinguish us from all other species. Both characteristics can be helpful or deadly, depending on the consequences we draw. First of all, we possess intelligence and technology; and secondly – as a result of these two features – our evolution, at least with regard to our own species, has been uncommonly successful.

The near future will prove how long this success will last. In any case, it is certain that continuous population growth is an exceedingly dangerous success, even if it exhibits a different dynamism from region to region.

Just as multiple agrarian cultures developed independently of each other, triggering different rates of population growth around the world, the continuing increase is occurring in different parts of the world in very dissimilar ways. While an end to this growth is clearly discernible in several industrialized countries, in other regions it is unlikely to occur very soon. This delay and the magnitude of any additional increase are of the greatest concern to all mankind.

A rapid end to this population increase and in the long term even a decline, first and foremost for ecological and social reasons, is probable and in principle possible – assuming that we now act accordingly.

Acting accordingly requires an unprejudiced view of the entire magnitude and complexity of the matter. A rapid end to the increase, followed by a gradual reduction of the human population, would not only improve prospects for the continued existence of a biosphere capable of supporting human life, but of the human species as well. This kind of development would particularly benefit the living conditions of the many human beings whose personal existence is by no means secure, but instead increasingly threatened.

The consequences of human overpopulation are becoming increasingly serious. Every additional person not only represents a competitor for the supply of food, but through his mere existence and his demands for a particular quality of life he unavoidably contributes to the further reduction of biodiversity and to many other threats to the environment.

Securing one's existence thus has two sides, one which is impersonal and refers to humanity as a whole, and the other which is related to sole individuals. The more people go hungry or starve, the further we distance ourselves from the specific human goal of securing each individual existence. Obviously we have long since exceeded the attainable optimum, i.e. a compromise between securing the existence of the species and that of all its individuals.

The Goal in Retrospect

First of all, we not only have to realize that the first two big goals – the foundation and securing of human existence – now lie behind us, but that a new problem is becoming more and more threatening: Ecosystems or parts of them can collapse, even without any human influence. Lakes that are insufficiently buffered by alkaline minerals and are exposed to a large amount of acid input (e.g. due to volcanic activity or combustion gases) can experience biological death within a very short time, such as a previously species-rich lake in Yellowstone Park whose sudden acid death is indicated by countless dead trees. A completely different example of a collapse is the migratory locust that brings about the end of its own overpopulation through mass reproduction and complete defoliation.

Both examples refer to events which thus far have been largely confined on a local scale in parts of nature not influenced by humans and have thus only affected small sections of the biosphere. The remaining abundance has usually remained untouched. Exceptions are rare but far-reaching natural catastrophes, such as volcanic eruptions, meteorite impacts or major floods. They have always had the potential to abruptly destroy a species-rich biotope, and in extreme cases even large parts of the entire biosphere.

Such disasters have occurred several times in the past and have radically influenced evolution through the extinction or recession of old species and the emergence or advancement of new ones. These events were acts of nature that humans neither influenced nor were able to and therefore they will not be given any further consideration within the scope of this book.

The situation has fundamentally changed, however, with the mass expansion of man throughout the entire biosphere. The distribution of humans is considerably greater than a swarm of locusts or hot sulfur springs and, as "omnivorous animals" and technicians, humans are substantially more effective than either one of them. Thus these examples have an alarmingly intimate correlation to our current situation. They cannot be taken seriously enough as warnings about the possible collapse of larger ecosystems due to the environmental damage caused by humans.

In reviewing the past we are able to ascertain that the phase of securing our existence was as important as reproduction, distribution, and the greatest possible control of natural (especially biological) threats. The main goal of survival of the species was instinctively determined, but not the point at which this goal would be reached. Only in retrospect do we realize that we have gone far beyond the mark.

It is impossible to determine just how far the goal of preserving our species lies behind us in any conclusive manner, or when the excesses began with which our population density, environmental pollution, and the constriction of the biosphere crossed critical boundaries — if only for the reason that every point of change is greatly dependent on our overall behavior. It makes a great difference, for example:

- as to whether we engage in a moderate or a wasteful lifestyle,
- how we value other species and individuals, especially in threatened biotopes such as tropical rainforests, tidal flats, flood plains, coral reefs, etc., and
- whether or not our practical actions are generally guided by ethical values.

More helpful than the exact determination of a position that has already been left behind is the question of how we arrived at such a sudden turning point; that is, how is it that humankind has become a menace to its own habitat in such a short period of time, compared to the length of its evolution?

Resolved and Unresolved Dangers

Every living creature has two reasons to counter physical threats. A genetically anchored instinct to maintain the species is combined with an equally instinctive will for individual survival. The existence of both the species and the individual is to a certain degree less threatened the greater the number of those collectively involved in warding off a threat – either through statistical reduction of the risk or through mutual assistance.

The physical threat to early humans had many faces, ranging from animals of prey, illness, hunger, adverse weather conditions, and rapid climate change to local and global natural catastrophes. Of these, illness, hunger, and natural catastrophes continue to be basic problems today.

Hunger and satiation are the central themes of this book. Illness and its prevention will also be dealt with extensively in one way or another, in humans as well as in plants. And with regard to major natural catastrophes, we will remain relatively powerless for the time being despite the increasing importance and reliability of predictions and early warning systems.

The danger posed to us by animals of prey has been coped with the most effectively. Many of them even run the risk of becoming extinct and have been reduced to a few harmless, but even more endangered, specimens in zoos, reserves, and inhospitable areas. Humans have taken over their biological role at the upper end of the food chain by being hunters and, what is more, destroyers of natural habitats. At the top of this chain, human beings have reduced biodiversity to a single – that is, their own – species. They are the victors in the competition among all large predators.

Invisibly small pathogens, whose nature as fungi, bacteria and viruses was first discovered by modern science, are found on the opposite end of the scale of menacing organisms. Despite enormous efforts, their eradication has by no means been successful. On the contrary: most of them were spread around the world along with our global expansion and recent mass tourism.

Even the World Health Organization's proclaimed eradication of the human smallpox virus in 1979 has now proven to have been wrong. Numerous pathogens have been disseminated more widely than ever before in the recent past and new ones have cropped up most easily in places where the density of human development offers favorable breeding grounds. Mass livestock farming, the rapidly increasing growth of huge cities around the world, a lack of hygiene and, above all, the rapid growth of slums in the city outskirts are exceedingly serious threats.

The Spread of Pathogens

The fundamental existence of pathogens cannot be questioned due to their close relationship to useful microorganisms. If we completely eradicated pathogens this would probably be synonymous with the end of a microbial diversity that guarantees two essential benefits: the natural turnover of all decaying organic matter, and the viability of those higher organisms that depend on their functional contributions (e.g. intestinal bacteria in humans and animals or the symbiotic fungi in the root zone of plants). Both of these functions are indispensable for a complete and healthy biosphere. Thus it would be illusory to attempt to completely eradicate pathogens, whether in humans, animals or plants. We would always affect useful microorganisms as well.

Theoretically it is conceivable to completely eradicate some particularly pathogenic viruses, and perhaps certain fungal or bacterial strains. Even if unsuccessful, the human smallpox virus represents the most famous example of this kind of attempt, although its host range was limited to humans. However, most pathogens are microorganisms (fungi and bacteria) that are closely related to a plethora of non-pathogenic forms. These relationships between pathogenic and non-pathogenic micro-organisms represent an extensive reservoir of harmless original forms that adapt to potential host organisms by way of natural mutation (spontaneous genetic change), becoming pathogenic.

The high mutation rates of microorganisms, caused in part by their short generation times (from minutes to days), provide the higher organism with hardly a chance to defend itself with the same means. Even if it was actually able to develop a suitable resistance through complementary mutation, it would almost always be too late because of the generally much longer genera-tion times of animals and plants (months to years).

The greater the genetic diversity of a potential host organ-ism, the lesser the probability of mutual contagion and prolifera-tion of a disease. Genetic diversity (biodiversity) manifests itself in both the richness of species and the low degree of relation-ship between the individual members of a species (avoidance of inbreeding). High biodiversity significantly reduces the ability of pathogens to cause diseases by limiting the population density of each particular species and its individuals.

Insofar as a species is able to survive at all in the dynamic balance of a biocoenosis, the optimum population density will develop as a function of the interdependency between the coexisting species and individuals. A biocoenosis consists of all organisms, including microbial pathogens, that have a regulating effect on this natural dynamic balance. In this respect each individual and each species contributes to the stability of the biocoenosis as long as their composition is regulated in accordance with biological principles. However, it is precisely this which has been less and less the case since the adoption of an agrarian lifestyle by humans.

The Turning Point: From Being Threatened by Nature to Threatening Nature Itself

The consequences of our increasing intervention in natural biocoenoses are serious. This is apparent in both the spread of pathogens and the rapidly changing living conditions with which nearly all other species within the entire biosphere now have to cope. This intervention occurs very effectively in various ways:

- through the continuous conversion of once extremely varied biotopes into mass cultures of a few domesticated species and their accompanying organisms;
- through the increasing pollution of large and small ecosystems with synthetic products that either fail to decompose at all or only do so very slowly, thus escaping the biological principle of growth and decomposition of all organic matter;
- through the lowering of the water table and salinization of soil in areas that are artificially irrigated, as well as various forms of water resource management (reservoirs, the channeling of rivers, the drainage of wetlands, etc.);
- through massive impact on local and global climates (the production of greenhouse gases, e.g. carbon dioxide and methane, as well as nitrogen oxides through the combustion

of fossil fuels, or methane through the cultivation of rice
and livestock farming [p. 216]; the clearing of forests which
serve as water reservoirs and sources of climate regulation;
soil erosion on mountain slopes or on dry and windy
cultivated fields).

Currently more than 1.5 billion hectares of the Earth's surface
are used for agricultural purposes. Approximately two-thirds of
this area is used as pastureland. The vast majority of our globally cultivated food and forage crops consists of a few species
of grain (wheat, rice, corn, and barley) as well as potatoes,
soybeans, sweet potatoes, and cassava. The stock of domestic
livestock (cattle, pigs, poultry, sheep, goats, and horses), trees
in forestry (spruce, fir, Douglas fir, and poplar), and fish in pisciculture (trout, salmon, perch, and carp) is equally one-sided.
Moreover, all of these cultivated plants and animals occur in
populations of genetically very closely related individuals from a
few species which would never have evolved in this form without
human intervention in a naturally developing biotope.

In addition to all the lavish treatment necessary for the maintenance of such unstable populations, they also require elaborate protection against pathogens and other pests. Wheat, corn,
and potato fields, cow pastures, pig and poultry batteries, trout
ponds, and spruce forests are not only the basis of human sustenance, but they are also a "bonanza" for countless pathogens
and many other natural enemies and consumers, from rooks,
pigeons, sparrows, rats and mice to locusts, bark beetles, and
aphids.

These types of mass culture, which do not occur in the realm
of untainted nature, are ideal experimental fields for the evolution of microorganisms; for instance the testing of mutations
for the improved adaptation of pathogens to new types of host

plants and animals. We are especially effective in increasing this dangerous potential even further by spreading pathogenic germs around the world with the frequency and speed of modern flight connections, in spite of all the attempted measures at quarantine.

The ambivalence of every type of development is also apparent here. From the point of view of their own evolution, humans have been extremely successful in the competition among the species. They have proven to be particularly superior to all those competitors and enemies among the animals of prey that threatened them in the beginning, and have either reduced their numbers to a point where they are no longer dangerous or have eradicated them completely. Humans have not achieved this by consciously using their intelligence and technology alone. A considerable part of this seeming success consisted in the immense increase in human population density and the demand for a steadily growing share of the commonly used habitat.

But because the number of humans and their domesticated plants and animals have increased so massively (not to mention pests and pathogens) and spread out in our limited habitat at the expense of other species and individuals, many other competitors in addition to animals of prey also had to move aside: predators are not the only threatened or extinct species – they are merely the clearly visible apex of the shrinking pyramid of life.

This list is even significantly incomplete as long as it only takes the inevitable biological displacement of many other species by humans into account. It does not consider the effect of human behavior patterns that extend far beyond the biological necessities and thus create additional ecological losses. The unrestrained consumption of luxury goods (furs, sea turtles, caviar, etc.) and poorly conceived technologies or those used for sports or entertainment are among the most common of these activities (the hunting of buffaloes, ostriches and other birds, etc.).

Even the unavoidable minimal impact that a population of more than six billion people has on the rest of the biosphere is threatening enough. This should be a sufficient reason to bring a swift end to this development. Securing our existence to a greater extent through existing means doesn't appear to be possible. On the contrary, ever since humans have exceeded an optimum population density they are no longer threatened by the natural world around them, but rather have themselves become a threat to it. Thus the goal of securing our existence – which on the whole we unconsciously and instinctively attempted to achieve – was not absolute, but instead only relative.

There can be no absolute security, neither for an individual nor for a species, nor – as is becoming increasingly apparent – for the biosphere as a whole.

Because evolution is not reversible and the history of human development cannot be repeated, the exact position of the turning point is of little importance. More important are the realization that this point has indeed been transgressed, and the willingness to draw the necessary conclusions.

Success breeds responsibility. The second phase of our own developmental history has inevitably made us the guardian of the entire biosphere of this Earth.

The Third Phase: Protection of the Biosphere

The fact that we are able to look back on the end of the second phase indicates that the third phase must have begun. A fitting sign of transition into the third phase consists in the ambivalent relationship between humans and pathogens. Pathogenic microorganisms and viruses that affect humans have of course always been present. And yet, the great plague pandemics that occurred in Europe during the 14th and 15th centuries were only as serious as they were because mobility, population density, and the concentration of people in urban settlements had decisively increased without the required attendant development in terms of hygiene. A population of animals living in such dense areas without intellectual and technological means would probably have been affected even more.

With the Enlightenment, the Scientific/Technological Revolution began in the field of medicine at an early stage, even if the specific treatment of infectious diseases did not commence until later. However, the beginning of the Scientific/Technological Revolution is just as difficult to determine as the beginning of the Neolithic Revolution. Both events were smooth transitions from an outdated to a progressive form of life. Just how fundamental and irreversible they were was not recognized until their complete breakthroughs had occurred.

The prevention and cure of illnesses represents an appropriate example of the transition to the third phase for two reasons. On the one hand, it demonstrates a great deal of scientific and technological progress while, on the other, underscoring the fact that completeness cannot be achieved. Today the causes of the plague and many other classical contagious diseases (tuberculosis, typhoid, cholera, etc.) have been largely brought under control, at least in industrialized countries. This has been achieved through inoculations, treatments with antibiotics and by fighting the carriers where applicable (rats and fleas in the case of the plague).

By contrast, the spread of viral infections that are difficult to treat (e.g. AIDS and influenza) has been nearly unchecked. The most serious influenza pandemic up to now was the "Spanish flu" in the winter of 1918/1919, which accounted for approximately twenty million deaths. The deadly consequences of the AIDS pandemic cannot be foreseen at present. The same applies to our farm animals and household pets (avian flu, for example), and similar problems with the diseases of our most important crops will constitute a major topic below.

At this point a fundamental observation may be appropriate: the consequences of the explosive growth of the human population have led to an increasingly unstable biological equilibrium that can only be maintained with resources from the Scientific/Technological Revolution. However, this is becoming increasingly risky, as a growing number of species become extinct or surrender their stabilizing role, thus leading to even greater instability.

> The conclusion can only be the demand to quickly and significantly reduce the size of the current population, even if this appears to be a utopian idea at present. After the phases of founding and securing human existence the third phase has to consist of replacing quantitative growth with qualitative progress.

In the long term, however, this goal is hardly utopian. It simply cannot be achieved immediately and it will require a great deal of effort in order to devise a tolerable transition phase. The qualitative principle has long been dominant in the biological evolution of the human mind and hand. Why should it not also play a greater role in determining our cultural evolution; that is, our cultivating (fostering and preserving) way of dealing with the natural world that surrounds and sustains us?

The Earth's population continues to increase dramatically (currently 80 million people each year). Hence, immediately before us lies the cultural and biological task of using science and technology not as an end in itself or as the aimless result of our development thus far, but as a tool for the optimum safeguarding of our biosphere. The precise course the population curve actually takes (if, when, to what extent, and under what circumstances it returns to a lower level) will be significantly influenced by the accomplishment of this task.

The Scientific/Technological Revolution was, and still is, as ambivalent as science and technology itself. The fact that social, economic, medical-hygienic, and medical-therapeutic conditions have so rapidly improved, especially in today's industrialized countries, has decisively helped individuals to live longer and healthier lives. The revolution has thus played a major role in the enormous population growth. And yet, it is the only effective means of repairing the existing damage as much as possible and in a sustainable manner, even if this calls for technologies that represent a considerable improvement over those employed up to now.

In this respect the Scientific/Technological Revolution marks the end of the second and, at the same time, the beginning of the third phase of our evolution. The success of this third phase will, among other challenges, be essentially dependent on whether we will be able to develop a sustainable and environmentally appropriate type of agriculture during the present period of a dangerously high – and yet increasing – population density.

Conflicting Aspects of Agriculture

Land, landscape, farmer, agro-economics, agriculture – an extremely conflicting mixture of terms and associations.

Land is (in addition to being a politically organized state) according to Meyers Encyclopedia either "The part of the earth's surface that rises above sea level," or a synonym for "land outside urban areas which is mostly used for agricultural purposes." (Note: the second meaning of the German word *Land* is 'countryside' in English). In the first case land covers the entire non-aquatic biosphere, in the second the same area with the exception of cities. Cities are thus either a part or the opposite of what makes them viable.

This implies an ambivalent interdependency. The more numerous and larger cities become, the more space for settlement areas and food production they require. The land or countryside thus pays the price of a city's existence. In addition, there is an ever-increasing intensity of land use for streets, railways, water and air traffic, as well as for all types of recreational activities. Just like settlements and agriculture, these areas also require predominantly fertile land at the expense of formerly species-rich natural biotopes. A view from an airplane onto human settlement areas reveals a striking picture of just how extensive the acquisition and use of land actually is (Fig. 2, color photograph I).

Landscape, in contradistinction to land as a whole, is the "name for a particular part of the Earth's surface which has unique characteristics as a result of its appearance and the interaction of its prevalent geological factors, thus distinguishing it from the surrounding area." Accordingly, landscape is something individual and unique. For this reason it has aesthetic and emotional as well as biological and economic values. We emphasize this through terms such as landscape painting, landscape design, landscape conservation, and landscape protection. Today nearly all landscapes with the exception of a number of deserts, steppes, savannas, jungles, and the Antarctic are cultural landscapes designed or influenced by humans. The majority is used for agriculture.

Farmers are people who not only cultivate the land, but "manage" it as well. They now find themselves caught between the conflicting priorities of cultural tasks and the production of food. Modern farmers have to think of themselves (once again according to Meyers Encyclopedia) as "managers." Contemporary job titles correspond to this definition: in Germany, depending on their education they are either master farmers, agricultural technicians, agricultural engineers, certified agricultural engineers, certified agricultural biologists, or certified agricultural economists. This not only indicates the changed social position attributed to today's farmers, but also the integration of agriculture in the dominating roles of economics, technology, and science.

As a result of this development, the agricultural sector in industrialized countries, which just a few centuries ago employed a large majority of the population, now employs no more than a small specialized minority. In Central Europe around AD 1800, 80% of the population was thus employed. Today this figure is less than 5%. Therefore, it is perhaps not surprising to note how little understanding there is on the part of the great majority for the increasingly important cultural and ecological tasks dealt with by farmers. This is expressed most clearly in the majority's flippant demand (independent of their social and economic situation) for high productivity, high quality, great diversity – and low prices!

Economics is the dominant point of view. The scale and importance of agriculture unquestionably makes it the most important sector of the world's economy. The structure and development of the economy with all of its complex global interdependencies thus affect every aspect of agriculture. Agriculture as a whole – and individual farmers even less and only under special circumstances (the "organic market") – cannot evade this situation. This fact is often neglected by those who rightly demand more environmentally compatible agriculture without realizing that this essentially requires a substantial change in basic economic conditions. Demands for change must be made on the political system and society first – especially on consumers – and only then on agriculture.

Agriculture is therefore part of an extremely complex structure that reflects social, economic, technological, and scientific changes since the time of their origin, the Neolithic Period. Each one of these aspects can be split up in various ways. This is especially true for science and technology, which have given modern agriculture a decisive impetus over the past few centuries. This is, in part, discussed in Chapter 2.

Much that began as a stimulus has in the meantime become an essential component. In addition to breeding, synthetic fertilizers and pesticides – the most important results of a scientific agrochemical sector – have played a major role in the enormous increase in agricultural yields during the 20th century. Thus they have become one of the basics of our diets around the world. Even more than the mechanization of planting, harvesting, and processing technologies (which more or less promote larger harvests and profitability, depending on the size and organization of the company, labor costs, the job market, etc.), chemical fertilizers and pesticides are almost always decisive factors in terms of yield and production costs.

This type of development also has two sides. Without agrochemicals six or seven billion people could not be fed; but their use has meant excessive pollution of many soils and bodies of water, and to an increasing degree the air as well.

Fertilization Against Soil Depletion

Fertilization is an important part of the agrochemical industry. Scientific insights into the fundamentals of plant nutrition gained by Humphrey Davy, Justus von Liebig and other agricultural chemists of the 19th century were not widely accepted at first. This, however, was only a matter of time, as the soils were leached out and depleted.

For almost one thousand years, from the end of the mass migration of European peoples in the 9th century up to the beginning of the 18th century, three-field crop rotation (winter grains – summer grains – fallow land) was the prevailing system of Central European agriculture. Nutrients depleted from the soil could not be sufficiently replaced by adding manure from domesticated animals, humus and plant residue from the woods or peat. The loss of soil fertility had to be compensated for through an expansion of agriculturally used areas. In addition, a temporary decline of the population in the late Middle Ages quickly changed into a population explosion in the modern era. Even then unfavorable locations like highlands, swamps, and coastal regions had to be turned into agricultural areas.

Not only were many soils soon leached out, but the limits of expansion had also been reached. A series of complementary measures was taken at the end of the 18th century and even more during the following century in order to intensify agricultural production on existing fields:

- Planting fallow fields with forage crops, mainly legumes to fix atmospheric nitrogen, which allowed for more livestock to be raised (clover, alfalfa, lupines, sainfoin, peas, and horse beans);

- the development of machines for working the soils, seeding, and harvesting (e.g. more intensive use of the soil by deepening the plow furrow, improved weed control through harrowing, in general greater working efficiency);
- supplementing organic fertilizers with mineral or mineralized fertilizers (lime, marl, niter, guano, wood ashes, and bone meal);
- the gradual transition to an improved three-field or crop rotation system (annual alternation of cereal crops and herbaceous plants: depending on the type of soil usually either potatoes, sugar beets, or forage beets).

Each of these developments was significantly promoted by the upswing of science and technology, especially in the areas of plant breeding, fertilization, and pesticides, and has been continuously improved up to the present time. New findings about the basic principles of plant metabolism provided for a substantially more targeted approach than before.

Plants differ from animals above all through their ability to transform light into chemical energy, and thus carbon dioxide from the air into organic substances (photosynthesis). With the exception of some microorganisms, all life on Earth is directly or indirectly dependent on this reaction. In no other metabolic reaction or chemical structure do plants differ to such a great extent from other forms of life. In principle, all organisms and their cells are similarly constructed. In addition to water, they all contain fat, numerous organic nitrogenous, phosphorous, and sulfurous compounds as well as potassium, sodium, calcium, magnesium, iron, copper, zinc, and other inorganic trace elements, all of which have to be ingested with food.

Plants are primarily nourished through their root systems while relying on the considerable assistance of various organisms in the soil. Some of these soil organisms, especially fungi, have a symbiotic, mutually beneficial relationship (mycorrhiza) with the plant roots.

Carbon dioxide and a limited amount of water are taken directly from the air by plants through small openings in the leaves. All other nutrients and a major part of the water come from the soil. Depending on its natural composition and on whether depletion through agriculture has already occurred, one or more nutrients will often be lacking, which in turn will limit growth. These have to be added back to the soil for optimal agricultural usage. For thousands of years this was done on the basis of practical experience with organic fertilizers, though the reason remained unknown.

Only since modern elementary analyses by agricultural chemists do we know that plants draw all of the basic elements for their complex make-up in mineralized (inorganic) form from the soil, except for carbon and oxygen, which are both derived from atmospheric carbon dioxide. In contrast to this purely inorganic source of nutrients, animals are completely dependent on plant or animal (thus indirectly plant) food sources. Hence the supposition that had prevailed from Aristotle's time up to the 18th century, purporting that plants receive their nutrients in organic form from the soil, turned out to be wrong.

The respective conditions for individually targeted plant nutrition through the use of precisely calculated mineral fertilization were provided by this new knowledge. Soil analyses revealed every deficiency, including trace elements. Individual nutrient requirements for every plant species could be determined and the fertilizer optimized accordingly. As long as enough water was available and healthy soil biology (bacteria, fungi, and small animals) provided favorable soil and the necessary nutrient turnover, growth and yield with optimum fertilization would only be limited by the plant's genetic constitution itself, and by the climate, competitors (weeds), and pests.

Because plants only require inorganic nutrients, synthetic compound fertilizers can be industrially manufactured on the basis of naturally occurring minerals and industrial waste products (slag lime, Albert slag). In contrast to all the remaining components of mineral fertilizers, suitable nitrogen compounds could at first only be obtained from Chile niter or guano.

The large-scale Haber-Bosch process of synthesizing ammonia from atmospheric nitrogen was therefore a significant breakthrough at the beginning of the 20th century. This provided large amounts of ammonium salts which are easily taken up by plants and used on a massive scale for nitrogenous fertilizers. However, a very high amount of energy is needed to manufacture ammonium and the environmental impact of energy production is becoming a bigger and bigger disadvantage. For this reason the special case of legumes, which do not require any nitrogen fertilization, is particularly interesting. As "nitrogen-fixing plants" in green manure (a cover crop) they satisfy their need for nitrogen indirectly from the air with the help of symbiotic bacteria (rhizobia) in root nodules.

The most important agricultural crops are not capable, however, of forming such structures and are therefore dependent on the supply of all nutrients, including inorganic nitrogen. The use of synthetic fertilizers is thus very costly, but also effective. They have become an essential factor in the productivity of agriculture and have played a significant role in the considerable increases in yields during the past few decades. Yet because of the simultaneous intensification of capital expenditures pressure grew to carry out precise cost-benefit analyses and to provide protection against growth and harvest losses caused by weeds, pests, and diseases.

Fighting Weeds

We call undesirable competitors for space, nutrients, water, and light in a field of crops "weeds". They have always been a natural attendant feature of agriculture. Most weeds have a considerable advantage over crops when it comes to growth, as crops are bred in a one-sided fashion for a particular type and amount of yield, a fact which impairs their natural ability to compete and renders them dependent on human maintenance.

Weeds are often characterized by rapid growth, great resilience, high propagation rates and long-lived seeds. The seeds of many weeds have a lifespan in the soil of several decades. The majority of weeds are native wild herbs and grasses that have adapted to the soil and climate conditions over long periods of time. Increasingly, however, ruderal plants (tough and adaptable "rubble plants") from other regions or continents and other crop companion plants are being introduced. Well-known examples of widely adaptable and globally disseminated "cosmopolitans" include dandelion and the bracken fern.

An important method of controlling weeds is a well-balanced crop rotation system that involves frequently changing methods of cultivation and thus constantly changing growing conditions for unwanted plants. An increasing simplification and standardization of crop rotation in contemporary agriculture (in EU countries cereals make up almost 80% of the total) does just the opposite, and creates conditions under which firmly established weed populations flourish. But even under more favorable conditions the cultivation of crops without sustained weed control measures is not conceivable either on a large scale (fields) or a small scale (gardens).

The oldest method of weed control that has been continuously improved over the millennia is the manual or mechanical removal either by hand or with hoes and harrows. During the last few decades this has been very efficiently complemented through the use of chemical weed control substances (herbicides). While this fundamentally new method has led to great increases in yield, it has also contributed considerably to the detrimental environmental factors of contemporary agriculture.

A tolerance of herbicides with minimal side-effects is therefore an important, if often misunderstood goal of plant breeding. A few selected examples of the application and impact of herbicides will help to understand the background.

Herbicides are synthetic chemicals whose use for weed control has been empirically determined by the extensive testing of millions of compounds. They have often been further optimized by modifying their chemical structure. Today a large number of substances with herbicidal effects are being used. They may or may not differ greatly in their chemical nature and their effects, but what they all have in common is their specific mode of action through which they harm plants more than other organisms. Together with insecticides, fungicides, and bactericides, etc., which selectively kill or impede the vitality of insects, fungi, and bacteria, herbicides (Latin *herba* = grass, weed, *-cide*, from Latin *caedere* = kill) are a type of biocide.

Depending on the type of application and the particular mode of action, herbicides are classified as either contact or soil-applied. Both work either selectively, affecting only certain types of plants, or non-selectively, killing all plant material with which they come into contact. The latter are referred to as total herbicides. Due to their effectiveness on all types of plants they are often used on railroad tracks, parking lots, and public paths, while in agriculture selective herbicides, which affect weeds more than crops, are used. However, what applies to antibiotics and other types of medicine also applies to herbicides: there is no such thing as an effector substance that has no side effects.

Agriculturally used herbicides thus have to be doubly selective: on the one hand, they must only work against plants, but not against the crops that are to be protected on the other. Damage to plants as opposed to other organisms is based on interfering with plant-specific reactions such as photosynthesis or other explicit features of plant metabolism. It is also possible to render weeds harmless before they begin to disseminate seed by inducing exaggerated growth and premature exhaustion through the use of "growth-promoting herbicides."

In agriculture, insensitivity to herbicides plays an important role. A comparatively insensitive plant is designated as being herbicide tolerant. The term *tolerance* is always used when the issue is insensitivity to non-biological stress factors, i.e. herbicides, salts, dryness, heat, cold, and all other types of chemical and physical stress. When referring to biological stress factors (pathogens, insects, or nematodes), *resistance* is referred to instead.

The selective tolerance of crops to synthetic chemicals is rare in comparison to other forms of tolerance for a simple reason: herbicides have only been used for a few decades as a form of plant protection. The adaptation of plants through the natural evolution of tolerance mechanisms has hardly begun in comparison to the resistance or tolerance to other threats which have existed for a long time; terrestrial plants have had more than 400 million years since the beginning of their evolution to develop appropriate protective mechanisms against them.

However, modern agriculture has created completely different conditions for many pathogens and pests that are by no means only detrimental.

Fighting Pathogens and Animal Pests

Just like humans themselves, massively propagated crops provide an enormous breeding ground for natural enemies. It is hard to imagine better conditions for the establishment and proliferation of quickly adaptable strains of plant pathogenic fungi, bacteria, and viruses than the mass cultivation of a few staple food crops. The same applies to insects and other small animals – often carriers of diseases – that disseminate as leaf, fruit, and root pests just as much as their host plants do (many viruses are exclusively transmitted by certain stinging or sucking insects). Some insects, spiders, mites, and nematodes (roundworms) have almost as short a generation time as microorganisms, i.e. almost as great an ability to mutate and overcome plant defense reactions.

In addition to one-sided mass propagation, the removal of toxins and disagreeable flavorings from food by plant breeders has also significantly contributed to the problem. This involves the very group of plant ingredients that play a major role in defending against pathogens and pests precisely because of these unpleasant qualities.

Every farmer and amateur gardener knows from experience about the scale of damage that can be caused by numerous microorganisms and small animals in fields and gardens. Examples of the most well-known damage are fungal diseases such as blight or scab, rolled-up and stunted leaves after a virus infection, or yield losses due to animal pests such as nematodes, snails, mites, aphids, potato beetles, and fruit flies or their larvae. In some regions locust swarms, the "scourge of Allah," are serious threats. Even in the warmer climatic zones of Central Europe they appeared in vast numbers during the last great infestation in 1873–74. Larger animals such as rodents and birds also compete with us for the harvest, especially for plants whose natural deterrence has been weakened by the removal of toxins.

Once again synthetic chemistry has led to the application of more or less selectively acting compounds: fungicides for fungi, insecticides for insects, acaricides for mites, nematicides for nematodes, special rat and mouse poisons, etc. Despite intensive research viruses remain especially difficult to control because they are not independent organisms and only reproduce within their host's cells, which are not supposed to be damaged when fighting against viruses.

In principle, what applies to weeds also applies here: chemical disease and pest control is the prevailing method which also uses substances that have turned out to be selectively effective in long series of purely empirical tests. As no substances are completely free of side-effects, and because selectivity is frequently very limited within individual groups of organisms (e.g. insects), pests and useful species are often equally affected. Examples of useful, or at least harmless, insects that have been affected include bees and butterflies, many of which are endangered – even if not for this reason alone.

The downside of the successes of chemical plant protection was the accumulation of toxic substances in different food chains, including that of humans, the development of tolerant populations of pests which are more and more difficult to control, and impoverishment of the microorganism flora and small animal life in the soil. The visible result is the one-sided overrepresentation of a few species. With several of the organochlorines that functioned as particularly powerful insecticides, for example DDT (dichlorodiphenyltrichloroethane), the disadvantages became so pronounced because they exhibit little chemical reactivity and are thus nearly non-biodegradable. Although widely used as highly effective contact poisons just a

few decades ago, they are now either strongly regulated or prohibited in most countries.

Valuable alternatives or supplements to chemical plant protection are the numerous methods of biological pest control
that have either less or no environmental impact. If they are
not among the more general principles of "ecological farming,"
these methods are based either on the utilization of natural
enemies of the pest organisms (for example, ichneumon wasps
whose larvae develop within aphids and thus kill them) or on the
so-called autocidal control methods which, for instance, involve
male mosquitoes that have been sterilized by irradiation. These
insects are then set free in order to prevent further reproduction of the natural population through unsuccessful mating.
These types of biological methods have the advantage of being
extremely selective, but until now have only been used in a few
particularly well-examined cases.

Ecologically oriented disease and pest control attempts to
consider all relevant factors that foster the preservation or resto-
ration of a species-rich biocoenosis as the most effective general
means to prevent individual pests from getting out of control.
This requires a balanced system of crop rotation, the avoidance
of large-scale monocultures and various supplementary measures of nature conservation, e.g. the planting or maintenance
of hedges, clean lakes, ponds, and other ecologically valuable
biotopes.

Birds that feed on grains or other crops are especially good
examples of just how close together the opposing goals of protecting agricultural yields and natural species diversity often are.
Essentially the same applies to bees or butterflies as opposed to
their harmful cousins in the insect world.

Nevertheless, in our context we have to stick to an unprejudiced analysis of the facts so that the discussion of the downsides

of the "chemicalization" of agriculture does not become one-sided and miss the point altogether. It is certainly beyond doubt that the use of chemical pesticides, together with chemical fertilizers and modern plant breeding, has played a decisive role in the huge increase in agricultural yields in the 20th century. Due to the population explosion, however, even this increase has seldom been large enough to keep pace: while there has nearly been a twenty-fold increase in wheat production since the beginning of the Neolithic Revolution, the human population has increased 600-fold during the same time period, or about thirty times as much.

Yield increases for other cereal crops and potatoes have been similarly high. The big discrepancy that remained between the increases in agricultural yields and the human population had to be compensated for mainly by increasing the area under cultivation. In the meantime, however, we have reached – if not gone beyond – the limits of what our biosphere will tolerate.

The limits of what is achievable with fertilization and chemical pesticides in the agriculturally most productive areas in Europe and North America can hardly be extended further. Theoretically, it would be possible to almost double current yields using the high-yield varieties now available with cultivation conditions that are optimal for the plants in every regard (fertilization, pesticides, climate, soil, and irrigation). For example, the top yield for winter wheat in favorable areas of Germany is currently about 100 dt (decitons) per hectare, whereas the average yield is about 60 dt per hectare.

But this does not take into account the price that would have to be paid for such an extreme accomplishment. Modern cultivars not only make the greatest demands on their environment for high yields, they have also lost much of the original vitality of their wild ancestors during the course of breeding. Top yields, synchronous maturity, high nutritional quality, an even stalk height and stiffness with cereals, or well-proportioned tuber shapes with potatoes, etc., are gained at the expense of other metabolic processes as well as genetic diversity. Most crops lose more and more of their natural ability to defend themselves and compete with wild plants as they produce greater yields.

To try and meet all of the conditions necessary to continuously achieve top yields of one or more staple crops would not only be unrealistic from an economic viewpoint, but would also be unacceptable for ecological reasons. The average yields we are now producing have already presented us with problems that are increasingly difficult to solve.

Fertilization and Protection of Plants: Intensive – Alternative – Integrated

In the past few decades an investment-intensive type of agriculture, above all in industrialized countries, has led to broadly standardized methods of farming with extremely one-sided systems of crop rotation and increasing mechanized specialization. As a result of excessive reduction in species diversity, and despite the intensive use of agrochemicals, some weeds, animal pests, and pathogens have spread greatly (e.g. Foxtail Grass, aphids, potato blight, and powdery mildew). Control measures are becoming more elaborate and also more questionable due to environmental impacts.

Such considerable structural and organizational changes were by no means caused by developments in crop farming (and stock-breeding) alone. Fundamental changes in the overall social and economic situation (the wage structure, migration to the cities, automation, economic concentration and globalization) have a major share. Feedback into the specific developments of farming, such as the breeding of new high-yield varieties, fertilization, and pesticides, has further aggravated this general trend.

For instance the use of automated combine harvesters first became possible and profitable through the combination of several different factors: a regional shortage of manpower, high labor costs, short-stalked cereals that do not break in storms or strong rain showers, as well as an extensive lack of weeds due to herbicides. Today one person using such a "robot harvester" is able to harvest two hectares per hour, from the mature stand of grain to sacks or tanks full of harvested crops. But this type of big investment requires an amortization which can only be achieved through rational management and intensive use. By far the most efficient way is to concentrate on a small number of mechanically harvested crops in a particular region and to share the machines.

This kind of intensification of agricultural production has additional consequences arising from the inevitable abandonment of smaller farms and the expansion of larger ones. Several small farms that generate many different products in comparably small quantities become a few large farms which specialize in the production, e.g. of cereals and sugar beets, vegetables, milk, eggs, beef, or pork, respectively.

Of all the various social and economic upshots of intensive agriculture, in our context the ecological effects are particularly significant. The indirect effects, which are often ignored, are also important, e.g. the environmental impact caused by large energy expenditures for long-distance (often air-conditioned) shipping of products or for the manufacturing of nitrogen-based fertilizers.

What was at first a prerequisite for the mechanization of the harvest as part of an intensified form of agriculture was then itself intensified for reasons of profitability. Effective chemical weed control was on the one hand an indispensable point of departure, but on the other hand became more and more elaborate and intensive due to the increase in mechanized harvesting, the standardization of crop rotation, and the spread of weeds that were difficult to control.

This vicious circle merely adds to the increasing global environmental impacts caused by chemical pesticides in combination with one-sided crop rotation and changes in the soil's nutrient composition as a result of leaching or unbalanced fertilization. From an ecological point of view this development entails the following serious consequences:

- *The reduction of natural biodiversity* through the massive direct and indirect promotion of a comparatively small number of crops, companion weeds, animal pests, and pathogens, as well as the direct and indirect impairment or extinction of many other species;
- *the toxic pollution* of soils, water bodies, and food, especially through the use of pesticides and nitrogenous compounds (the latter partially from the concentrated liquid manure fertilization common to factory farming);
- *eutrophication* (the over-supply of nutrients such as phosphate and nitrogenous compounds), especially of standing and slowly flowing bodies of water with the result that algae and zooplankton grow excessively, reducing the oxygen available for higher animals.

Increasing consciousness of this problem has now led to various suggestions for improvements and to the testing of alternative methods ("close to nature," "biodynamic," "organic-biologic," and "alternative"). They are all aimed at:

- avoiding the use of synthetic pesticides as much as possible;

- controlling weeds, animal pests, and pathogens with a coordinated program of crop rotation and nutrient supply as well as through a special concern for climatic and soil conditions;
- fertilizing carefully, mainly employing organic fertilizers (manure, nitrogen-fixing plants as rotation crops, etc.) as well as natural mineral fertilizers (rock flour, slag lime, rock phosphate, etc.);
- working the soil in such a way that the soil biota is impaired as little as possible.

Every sensible and practicable suggestion for ecological improvements in agriculture has a dual effect: in general it promotes the development of a better awareness of the environment and in more specific terms, suitable action to this end, e.g. in private gardens and public facilities (as long as it doesn't become dogmatic and have the opposite effect). In this way it helps to achieve necessary changes in present practice in numerous critical areas where the intensive use of land is simply no longer tolerable: in biotopes and landscapes which are particularly worthy of protection, in water protection areas and in areas where there is a long-term threat to the groundwater.

To what extent the alternative methods of environmentally compatible agriculture are able to influence conventional methods of intensive land use in view of the increasing bulk production of staple foods must remain an open question, above all because of the unabated growth in population. Efforts to introduce extensive improvements while maintaining a sufficient amount of food production have now been consolidated in the concept of *integrated plant protection*. The goal of this concept is the qualitative improvement and combined application of all sensible biological, mechanical, and chemical methods to prevent crop or yield losses with due respect for ecological concerns.

The fact that ecological considerations are of vital importance and yet can only be a compromise in view of human overpopulation has been amply discussed. The question of whether the breeding of new varieties will help achieve the double goal of improved food production and environmentally compatible plant protection thus becomes even more important.

Summary

With reference to the environment, past human history can be divided into three phases whose transitions are marked by the Neolithic and the Scientific/Technological Revolutions. The first phase involved the founding of human existence while the second was concerned with securing it. We presently find ourselves in a decisive stage of the third phase with overriding emphasis on securing a biosphere that tolerates and sustains a dangerously large human population.

Providing adequate amounts of food for human consumption requires that our crops themselves are sufficiently nourished and protected from weeds, diseases, and animal pests. To this end, scientific and technological advances have led to considerable increases in yield, but have also resulted in environmental impacts that are no longer acceptable. Agriculture has to be brought into line with substantially improved environmental protection. This requires due consideration of ecological concerns, including improved integration of chemical, mechanical, and biological methods of fertilization and plant protection. Plant breeding is expected to play an important role in achieving this goal.

4 Crop Plant Breeding

Breeding is the use of the genetic potential for specifically directing the evolution of naturally occurring species in order to achieve a particular purpose, e.g. improvement of the quality and yield of food. The history of crop plant breeding most probably began with lentils, peas, barley, and the precursors of wheat (einkorn wheat and wild emmer). Soon after the cultivation and domestication of crops had become a new component of cultural evolution, more and more food crops and other kinds of use were incorporated. By approximately 1500 BC cultivated forms of almost all crops now used around the world had been developed.

Today we classify an almost overwhelming abundance of crops in several large groups according to their type of use: food, fodder, industry, luxury products, spices, ornamentals, medicinal products, and forestry. Plants grown for industrial purposes alone are further classified according to their vastly different utilizations as wood, fiber, cellulose, starch, rubber, cork, oil, resin, tannic acid, and dye. The range of uses for plants in the other groups is no less varied.

In principle, the following outline of the possibilities and limits of plant breeding applies to all crops. I will nonetheless limit myself to discussing food crops, with a few exceptions, in order to stay within the scope of the subject, i.e. our existential basic needs. As far as technical terms are unavoidable, I will explain them in the course of the text as well as in a glossary in the book's appendix.

Requirements of Our Diet

In the first instance breeding goals with crops are oriented toward our need for a diet which is quantitatively *and* qualitatively sufficient. Every breeding goal is therefore doubly limited by hereditary factors and the limits of their variability. In addition to the genetically specified traits of a particular plant, the likewise genetically specified nutritional requirements of humans play an equally important role.

Bread, one of our main sources of food, is a suitable example: in contrast to many plant-eating animals, humans cannot utilize cellulose – a main ingredient of the green parts of plants – as food due to our genetic constitution (even if it has an important function as roughage). Starch, on the other hand, which is a chemically similar carbohydrate, is easily digested by humans.

As the main ingredient of wheat flour and other cereal products, starch is not only a qualitatively valuable source of food, but is quantitatively the most important one as well. This is one of the reasons why we will take a closer look at the breeding history of wheat and a few additional cereals. And yet, starch alone is not a sufficient source of food. Many other components are necessary for balanced nutrition.

This brings us to another distinctive feature of the human genetic constitution (with certain deviations this applies to other higher animals as well). In order to remain healthy our body needs – in addition to water and mineral salts – more than just those organic nutritional components that can be digested by the stomach and intestines, taken up and transported by the blood, and then transformed by the liver into the body's own substances. We are also dependent on the regular intake of "essential" amino acids, fatty acids, and vitamins. Even though only small quantities of these compounds are needed, the human body cannot synthesize them itself, in contrast to many other metabolic products, and reacts to their absence in its diet by exhibiting signs of malnutrition. A long-known example is scurvy as a result of vitamin C deficiency.

Modern nutritional science has contributed substantially to a more precise definition of breeding goals for providing an optimum quality of food. Knowledge about the role that a balanced diet plays in avoiding malnutrition is not new. A one-sided diet of corn leads to a lack of the essential amino acids lysine and tryptophan; and of rice to a lack of vitamin A (poor eyesight and immunodeficiency), vitamin B_1 (beriberi), mineral trace elements, iron (anemia), zinc, and iodine, as well as to a lack of several essential amino acids.

Because of the large numbers of people affected, deficiency diseases caused by a one-sided diet of rice, often aggravated by insufficient amounts, are particularly alarming. Every year in African and Asian developing countries this leads to millions of people going blind and to the death of large numbers of children and young women. Therefore, this issue plays an important role in Chapter 6.

The human body has a physiologically, or ultimately genetically, determined need that is the vital criterion for the quality of food. This includes sufficient amounts of:

- usable basic organic nutrients (carbohydrates, fats, proteins),
- all of the inorganic nutrients required by the body (mineral salts, trace elements),

Table I   Important goals of crop plant breeding on the basis of
             genetically determined characteristics

Starch content
Content and quality of proteins
Content and quality of fats and oils
Other essential foodstuffs
Photosynthetic efficiency
Fixing of atmospheric nitrogen
Resistance to
    pathogens
    insect pests
Tolerance of
    herbicides
    drought
    salt
    heat
    cold
Uniform habit
Uniform maturation of fruit
Absence of toxins and unfavorable flavorings

- all essential organic substances (all vitamins, several amino acids and fatty acids),
- suitable roughage for the intestinal tract.

In addition, all food has to fulfill the following requirement:

- be free of toxins and unpleasant flavorings (both when raw and after being prepared).

Besides these fundamental demands for nutritional quality and the greatest possible yield, low-priced cultivation and processing as well as consideration of environmental criteria are the most important breeding goals. A selection of these goals is shown in Table 1. Their actual attainment depends on the variability of the plant's genotype selected for breeding.

Genetic Variability

According to Darwin's theory of evolution every plant – as well as every other organism – is a life form that has adapted to its particular environmental conditions over a long period of time. The outward appearance of every species created in this way represents a multi-faceted compromise between the countless new possibilities that arise from random mutation and the diverse limitations that structural and functional requirements place on the entire organism.

A very general example can serve as an explanation: A plant's function, form, size, and quantity of flowers, fruit, leaves, stems, and roots are, within certain limits, exactly harmonized with one another. The root system maintains and supports the plant while absorbing water and nutrients from the soil. Its width, depth, branching structure, and metabolic activity have to be optimally adapted to the soil composition (structure, water supply, and nutrient content) as well as to the needs of the parts of the plant above ground (nutrient turnover, weight, wind load, and evaporation). The same is true for all other organisms within typal boundaries.

A certain degree of adaptability to the prevailing environmental conditions is essential, e.g. to compensate for variations in climate, intensity and quality (spectral composition) of light, and soil conditions. Examples of astonishing differences in root depth or shoot length within the same species are generally well-known: Many plants grow deep roots in dry or nutrient-depleted

soils, or long shoots in the dark, until they reach water and nutrients or suitable light conditions. The limits of this kind of adaptation are either structurally determined, due to the necessity of
a balanced structural coordination of all parts of the plant, or
functionally by the maximum metabolic performance which can
be mobilized for disproportionate growth of individual organs.
This has important consequences for breeding:

- Although the disproportionate size of the harvested part
  of the plant (fruit, leaf, tuber, root, etc.) in comparison to
  the remaining organs is a primary breeding goal, it can only
  be achieved to a certain extent and is inevitably attained
  at the expense of metabolic performance in other regards.
  When looking at a giant pumpkin (a berry) or a cauliflower
  (reprogrammed inflorescence) it is easy to imagine just
  how much everything else had to be put on the "back
  burner" to achieve such a one-sided channeling of nutrients
  and solar energy into the production of a single greatly
  disproportionate organ. This necessarily limits many other
  capacities, including the resistance to pathogens, pests and
  many other types of stress.
- A high rate of growth requires a suitable supply of nutrients,
  intensive plant protection, and other optimal conditions,
  such as temperature, light, and water supply. As a rule rapid
  growth is achieved at the expense of general hardiness.

In this context a comparison of the terms *plasticity* and *variability* with regard to the responsiveness of a plant's genetic information may be helpful. Although the terms are not always clearly
distinguished from one another, the following definitions should
provide the necessary clarity.

Plasticity (adaptive modification) is the adaptability of a

plant's growth and other metabolic activities to its environmental conditions; that is, the flexible use of the genetic information fixed in the genotype, e.g. the adaptation of shoot length or root depth to local site conditions. By contrast, variability (genetic diversity or modifiability) is the inherited, individual genetic difference or differentiation potential within a species, e.g. different flower color or cold tolerance within the same plant species, or different eye and hair color in humans.

Plasticity and variability therefore use the genetic potential in different ways: plasticity is the ability to adapt the given genetic constitution to different environmental conditions, whereas variability describes individual differences and the changeability within the genetic constitution of a species.

The evolution of crops induced by breeding is based – just like the natural evolution of species and their individuals – on the variability of the genetic information. Plasticity then determines the different possibilities of using this information, including a crop's yield in a particular prevailing situation.

Figs. 16 and 17 (color plates II and III) each illustrate five different examples of the potential of genetic variability in plant breeding. The first case concerns five closely related species from the Solanaceae family (Fig. 16, color plate II), each of which has one of four different organs particularly emphasized by breeders: the petunia's flowers, the tobacco plant's leaves, the pepper and tomato plants' fruit, and the potato's tuber. One characteristic organ has been bred to an extreme form in every one of these species.

There are numerous genetic variations (varieties or cultivars) within all five species. For instance, the flowers, leaves, fruit or tubers may differ to a certain extent in color, shape, size, taste, water content, composition of nutrients, shelf life, adaptability to machine harvesting, etc. And yet, there are no potato or tomato varieties that have edible fruit *and* edible tubers, and no other double use occurs within the five species – with the exception of one curiosity which, however, does not contradict this principle: Potatoes in Europe were first valued as ornamental plants in royal gardens because of their beautiful flowers before their tubers became a staple food in the 18th and 19th centuries.

The breeding of crops is always concentrated on a particular organ of interest which may exhibit extreme morphological changes when compared with the original wild type. These kinds of metamorphoses are especially conspicuous with several species in the Brassicaceae family (Fig. 17, color plate III) that are once again closely related to each other: with cauliflower we use the extremely enlarged and compressed inflorescence, from rapeseed the oil from the seeds, from white and red cabbage the leaves, from kohlrabi the swollen stem, and from the rutabaga (yellow turnip) the main root which has been transformed into a storage organ. There are even a growing number of cabbages that are used as ornamental plants, which often vary greatly in color, shape, and size.

These types of examples can be found in many plant families. Every list, regardless of how detailed, has to remain incomplete, however, in light of the immense diversity of crops that have been domesticated during the millennium-long history of breeding and purposefully influenced in their continuing human goal-oriented evolution.

The Origins of Our Most Important Crops

The botanic and geographic origins of our crops are not certain in all cases. It is possible, however, to trace most of the important crops back to their original wild ancestors with a fair bit of accuracy. In doing so it becomes obvious that there are preferred areas of origin within which the wild types appear in populations of particularly large genetic diversity. Usually domestication has already begun in these "centers of diversity" (also referred to as "gene centers"). Fig. 18 shows the areas of origin for a selection of important crops. Almost all of them are now being cultivated in many different regions around the world, as far as climate and soil conditions permit.

Adaptation to conditions in different locations through the breeding of suitable varieties has always been an important goal of plant breeding. Even today these "gene centers" have great importance as sources of starting material for the breeding of new varieties. Some of the wild types native to these areas offer traits that are no longer present or are indistinct in the highly bred varieties used in current agricultural areas (e.g. genes responsible for specific disease resistances).

The especially large genetic diversity of the original flora and fauna is a result of the diversity of environmental conditions in individual regions in such centers. Different climatic and soil conditions in neighboring mountain valleys, high plateaus and flood plains put different kinds of selective pressure on separate populations of the same species.

To prevent possible irreparable losses, e.g. as a result of environmental damage, hundreds of thousands of seeds have been collected and stored as gene resources ("gene bank") in numerous international research institutes belonging to the FAO (Food and Agriculture Organization of the United Nations). A large proportion of these seeds originated from the gene centers shown in Fig. 18. They are available to plant breeders as source material for new varieties.

In addition to the breeding goals listed in Table 1, another important goal is the adaptation of crops from different sources

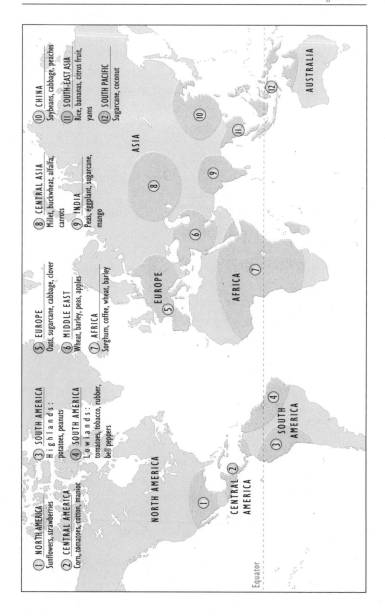

① NORTH AMERICA
Sunflowers, strawberries

② CENTRAL AMERICA
Corn, tomatoes, cotton, manioc

③ SOUTH AMERICA
H i g h l a n d s :
potatoes, peanuts

④ SOUTH AMERICA
L o w l a n d s :
tomatoes, tobacco, rubber,
bell peppers

⑤ EUROPE
Oats, sugarcane, cabbage, clover

⑥ MIDDLE EAST
Wheat, barley, peas, apples

⑦ AFRICA
Sorghum, coffee, wheat, barley

⑧ CENTRAL ASIA
Millet, buckwheat, alfalfa,
carrots

⑨ INDIA
Peas, eggplant, sugarcane,
mango

⑩ CHINA
Soybeans, cabbage, peaches

⑪ SOUTH-EAST ASIA
Rice, bananas, citrus fruit,
yams

⑫ SOUTH PACIFIC
Sugarcane, coconut

NORTH AMERICA

CENTRAL
AMERICA

SOUTH
AMERICA

EUROPE

AFRICA

ASIA

AUSTRALIA

Equator

Table 2 General breeding goals in addition to the specific goals listed in
         Table 1

High yield
Nutritional quality
Compatibility with local conditions
Shelf life
Specific forms of resistance and tolerance
Improved methods of cultivation
Improved methods of processing

to different climatic conditions, ecological circumstances, and
methods of cultivation, as well as to processing techniques and
eating habits. Some of these are explained in more detail in
the following chapters using selected examples. When summarized in general (Table 2), the principle directions taken by the
breeding of crops since the beginning of their use in agriculture
become apparent.

In pursuing these goals the Scientific/Technological Revolution has brought great methodological progress, even though
much had already been achieved through deliberate or accidental
selection for desired traits.

Breeding by Selection: An Ancient Method

A farmer who does not acquire his seeds through trade practices
breeding by selection: He chooses a part of the harvest to use for
the cultivation of next season's crop. This is either a conscious

Figure 18 Major centers of diversity, from which a majority of today's
           food plants originate (selected examples)

or an unconscious choice. As a rule a deliberate choice is more effective as far as breeding is concerned, but even an unconscious choice will lead to a change – a new variety – in the initial population after several repetitions. As an example let us look at a fictional case which might have occurred in this or similar fashion during the early phases of agriculture:

The scene of the event could have been a natural stand of barley located somewhere in the area of the Fertile Crescent. For many years it was harvested in the late summer by people from a nearby settlement. After a time the villagers noticed a decline in the yield and learned to compensate for the loss by sowing a portion of the harvest. This had to occur on time before the ears fell apart, and contained a mixture of mature and immature kernels. Both were suitable for eating, but when planted only the mature kernels developed. Their early and simultaneous maturity was part of the genetic predisposition within the limits of natural variability. It was inherited by most individuals in the next generation and was therefore more strongly represented in the following year. Thus, an initially mixed population that matured over a wide time-span gradually developed into a more and more uniform population of early maturing individuals.

Traders from this small community, whose new variety of barley was presumably a valuable object of exchange, could have offered another community located in a higher-lying mountain valley its kernels in trade for raw material for grindstones. Through this trade the new variety was introduced to a rougher mountain climate where winter hardiness became an additional criterion of selection. The outcome is easy to picture: A new variety of early maturing and winter hardy barley developed as a result of this twofold selection procedure.

All subsequent changes followed the same principle, which in the end is based on exploitation of the genetic variability within naturally occurring populations. Numerous cultivars, which to some extent had strongly divergent characteristics, arose in this manner over the course of many steps of what was at first the unconscious and then deliberate breeding by selection of every edible wild plant suited for domestication. Several specific examples will illustrate the wide range of possibilities in more detail below.

After thousands of years of successful application this breeding method was raised to a substantially more efficient level through scientifically based cross-breeding at the beginning of the 20th century. By this time all our staple food crops had long become cultivars which were no longer able to compete with the original wild types in nature. Without breeding (target-oriented genetic modification) and human maintenance the evolution of these plants would not have occurred.

Cross-breeding: Applied Genetics

While breeding by selection deals with individuals that are already present in a given population, cross-breeding aims at deliberately creating individuals with combinations of traits which did not exist before. For example, the hypothetical case of the breeding of an early maturing and winter hardy barley just described is only realistic if the genetic information for both traits was initially present in at least one individual and inherited by a sufficient number of progeny to start a new population.

If the combination of traits is not existent from the outset, breeding by selection can at best provide favorable selection conditions after their random emergence as a result of natural crossing or mutation. In contrast deliberate cross-breeding strives to specifically develop new varieties by combining traits that first appeared in different individuals.

The scientific basis for this new and considerably more specific process was a new branch of biology: genetics. Its founder was the Augustinian monk Gregor Mendel. The genetic laws and later on the mechanisms of gene function derived from his and subsequent crossing experiments are of such great importance to an understanding of this book that I will briefly summarize the basic assertions.

Every living entity, and in the case of multicellular organisms almost every cell, contains all genetic information in the form of thousands of genes, each of which carries a hereditary factor. The sum of all these genes, the *genome*, determines the *genotype*, which together with the changeable environmental influences determines the overall appearance, or the *phenotype*, of an individual.

The extent to which individual beings differ in their genetic makeup depends on their degree of kinship. Within the plant kingdom, for example, all members of the Solanaceae family illustrated in Fig. 16 (color plate II) are much more closely related than they are to a member of any other family, e.g. the Brassicaceae, to which the different types of cabbage species in Fig. 17 (color plate III) belong.

Asexual reproduction, for instance through grafting or cuttings, results in genetically identical individuals, or *clones*. Sexual reproduction (including deliberate cross-breeding), on the other hand, always results in a random mixture of parental genes, and thus in genetically different individuals.

With sexual reproduction the closest relationship exists between parents and their offspring, and between siblings. Statistically speaking, in these cases half of all the genes are identical. The fact that the paternal and maternal genes differ from one another (often recognizable by the phenotype, e.g. flower or eye color, or other visible hereditary traits) leads to a random mixture and a different genotype for every descendent.

In other words: every individual and every possible combination of genes that has actually occurred is unique. In the entire history of the Earth this cannot be repeated for two different reasons. Firstly, the statistical probability that exactly the same random mixture of two times many thousands of genes occurs is infinitely slight. Secondly, spontaneous mutations in individual genes as well as changes in their relative positions in the genome occur with low but finite frequency.

Either kind of mutation during cell division can affect every gene: all genes and genomes change slowly, randomly, and steadily. Over the approximately 400 million years which we assume that it took for the evolution of higher terrestrial plants, this genetic drift enabled those species now alive to continuously adapt as demanded by their changing environmental conditions ("survival of the fittest"). On the other hand, the mutations were seldom enough to ascertain the boundaries between existing as well as newly evolving species.

Despite their genetic uniqueness, all individuals of the same species are so similar in all essential traits, and so dissimilar to all other species, that the species is clearly defined. Apart from rare, but for plant breeding nonetheless important exceptions, species boundaries are therefore easily recognized as natural crossing barriers. As a rule this is also true within families and genera so that, for example, potatoes and tomatoes, or wheat and barley cannot be crossed with one another.

The chemical nature of the gene was not known in Mendel's day and state of scientific knowledge. In the meantime we have very detailed knowledge about the structure and function of genes which, as the foundation of genetic engineering, will be discussed in the next chapter. The practical application of Mendel's laws in the cross-breeding of new *cultivars* (= *varieties*) was already a first type of "genetic engineering," although this term had not yet been created for this newly developed breeding method.

Nevertheless, cross-breeding not only opens up new opportunities, but has clear limits as well.

Possibilities and Limits of Cross-breeding

Cross-breeding is at the same time practical application and basic research. A gene's predictable and ideal behavior according to Mendel's laws is a rare exception in the practice of breeding, mainly for two biologically important reasons. Firstly, crossing partners not only differ in just one particular gene that is responsible for a desired trait. Many additional differences in the genetic constitution of an individual always influence each other with regard to the type and intensity of their expression. Secondly, a particular trait is seldom influenced by one gene alone.

One of the rare cases of *monogenic* inheritance (based on a single gene) is the color of the pea blossoms with which Mendel carried out his experiments. Mendel was either extremely lucky, exceptionally intuitive, or both. In contrast to his chosen conditions, most traits that are of interest to a breeder are *polygenically* inherited (by more than one gene).

The professional breeder is thus always a researcher as well. With each new crossing he searches for preferential or optimal combinations of traits in the progeny in a practicably applicable form. However, he not only investigates the characteristic behavior and interdependence of genes during sexual reproduction. In so doing he always finds out something about the "genetic background" of the individuals he investigates, i.e. which additional genetically determined traits are present in a usable form in crossing partners, and which are missing.

The result of each breeding approach (the creation of a new variety with a specific combination of traits) is necessarily a strongly standardized genotype and thus represents a reduction of the original range of variation. Breeding is an attempt to emphasize a desired combination of traits in one genotype; for example, in a high-yielding, early maturing, winter hardy, tough-eared, naked (no spelt), herbicide-tolerant, and possibly also mildew-resistant wheat variety. This inevitably involves the reduction in intensity or even the complete loss of other traits that were present in the original population but which the breeder had to consider as less important.

In principle, cross-breeding makes it possible to combine outwardly perceptible as well as invisible species-specific traits from crossing partners in a new variety. One basic condition must be fulfilled, however: The traits have to find a suitable genetic background that allows for an expression in the desired mode and intensity. The suitability of a particular genotype for proper expression is only predictable to a certain degree as our knowledge about the underlying mechanisms is still very limited.

For the time being expression of a desired trait is predominantly a rule of thumb and has to be realistically tested in each individual case. The breeder does not normally know how important a single gene is in the interplay of all the genes that are involved in the expression of a complex trait (e.g. winter hardiness or drought tolerance). What counts is the final result: the intensity as well as the appropriate timing and location of expression.

A second condition for the combination of traits through cross-breeding (apart from a suitable genetic background) is the sexual compatibility (crossability) of the source individuals. This is, with a few exceptions, only possible within a species. Just as many plant species prevent incest through the sexual incompatibility of closely related individuals of the same species, most species are also protected from cross-hybridization through effective mechanisms of sexual incompatibility at the interspecies level.

A few exceptions to this "hybridization barrier" lead to *interspecies hybrids* which, however, in the case of animals usually produce sterile progeny (e.g. hinnies or mules as interspecies hybrids of horses and donkeys). Hybridization barriers are less strictly adhered to with plants than with animals. Intergeneric or interspecies hybrids capable of reproduction may indeed be created this way, but few of them play an important role in breeding (pp. 110ff.).

Cross-breeding is, with the above exceptions, only possible within natural species boundaries. Knowledge of which mechanisms play a role in the formation of, and adherence to, sexual incompatibility between species is still quite incomplete. For the continuing discussion it is important to note that transgression of these barriers in cross-breeding is very rare. By contrast, in gene technology-assisted breeding the possibilities are, in principle, unlimited.

Breeders are researchers in more ways than one. They search for and analyze the possible combinations of traits that are more or less different for every randomly created genotype; and in doing so they find out whether a particular trait has been transmitted in accordance with Mendel's law through a single "operationally" defined gene, i.e. through the operation of breeding. Polygenic inheritance of traits is more common, however, and is based on more complex transfer mechanisms.

The operational definition of genes according to breeding

results was a significant prerequisite for today's substantially more detailed analysis of individual genes using the methods of molecular biology as well as their transfer by way of genetic engineering.

Genetic research was also greatly enhanced by the possibility of triggering mutations artificially. Suitable chemical or physical *mutagens* (= mutation triggers: natural or synthetic substances; high-energy radiation) can significantly increase mutation rates. Inherited changes to the genetic information no longer appear with a low natural frequency, but instead with a frequency that is increased by several orders of magnitude (one mutation in 100 genes instead of one in 100,000 or a billion). If a particular trait in an individual no longer appears, then it is most likely that a mutation has affected the responsible gene.

It is not only possible to deactivate previously active genes by triggering artificial mutations, but inversely to activate inactive ("silent") genes as well. Although this second case is less common, the sum of both possibilities allows for a significant extension of the natural range of genetic diversity. This method has been practically applied in *mutation breeding* for decades.

So much for the possibilities and limits of cross-breeding. It has not made selection superfluous, but has integrated it so thoroughly in a new science-based concept of plant breeding that the selection of random results has been replaced by the targeted design of combined traits.

That the fruitful interaction of this new breeding method with major changes in planting and harvesting technologies, plant nutrition, and plant protection resulted in the great increases in yields in the 20th century has already been mentioned. The following examples should help to explain some important achievements and features of plant breeding in more detail.

Cereals as an Example

Since the beginning of agriculture in the Neolithic Period cereals have been the most important crops in terms of human consumption. There are a number of reasons for this special position. The fruit (kernel) is highly nutritious, can be stored for a long time due to its low water content, and can be prepared and eaten in various ways. Most cereals, especially wheat, corn, and barley, turned out to be extremely adaptable to different climatic and soil conditions during domestication. In comparison to many other crops they are undemanding in cultivation, care, and yield, and have a high yield per hectare. They are also relatively resistant to pests and able to compete with weeds.

In descending order of the quantity of harvest wheat, rice, corn, barley, oats, sorghum, rye, and millet are the most important types of cereal grains. The first three on the list are by far our most extensively cultivated sources of food.

The oldest domesticated crops are quite probably barley as well as einkorn and emmer, the now rarely cultivated ancestors of wheat. The long breeding history of these kinds of cereals allows us to trace a series of important goals and results of crop breeding. Fig. 18 has already shown us that these plants originated from the centers of diversity in the Fertile Crescent and in adjacent areas in North Africa and Central Asia.

The wild ancestors of our current barley and wheat crops had brittle ear axes. Under natural conditions this helps the plant to disseminate its kernels. Fig. 19 shows how the ears of wild forms fall apart at predetermined breaking points upon ripening, allowing each kernel to be carried away individually by the wind, insects and birds, or by other animals when the grains become attached to their fur. This natural goal of optimal dispersal contrasted with human aspirations for an easy and rich

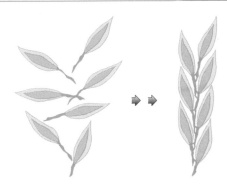

Figure 19 Schematic illustration of the change from brittle (left) to tough
ears (right), which occurred in all major cereal crops through
spontaneous mutations in the initial phase of domestication

harvest. That is why mutations that produced tough axes, which
apparently occurred early and spontaneously and allowed for a
harvest of mature kernels in intact ears, were a decisive step in
the domestication of barley and wheat.

It would not be hard to incorporate the new achievement
of tough ears and their preferred selection by humans in the
above-mentioned description of the selection breeding of an
early maturing and winter hardy variety of barley (p. 100). If we
further complement the age-old procedure of selecting favorable
traits with a superior readiness to germinate, an upright growth
habit, stem-solidness, disease resistance, high yield (as well as the
high quality needed for baking, brewing, and fodder) and simple
processing, e.g. the easy separation of the kernel from the glume
through the threshing of "naked barley" or "naked wheat," then
the big difference between the original wild forms and today's

Figure 20 Comparison of a wild
relative and a modern
high-yielding barley
cultivar

cultivars becomes apparent. Fig. 20 illustrates two such distant
varieties of barley.

Under the most favorable conditions it takes at least five to
ten years to produce a new variety with an additional, previously
lacking trait and to get it through the approvals process. It often
takes much longer than this.

Wheat: A Natural Hybrid

Wheat is not only our most important food plant, but also a
good example of a complex breeding history on the basis of up
to three independent natural hybridization events. The present-
day wheat cultivars are einkorn, emmer, durum wheat, spelt, and

common wheat. Of these, durum and common wheat are by far the most important for human nutrition.

Durum wheat is the preferred basic raw material for pasta, pearl barley, and semolina, whereas common wheat is used above all for the baking of bread and as fodder. Wheat starch, wheat beer, grain spirit, and whiskey are produced using particular varieties of wheat specially developed for these purposes.

Some species of wheat hybridize naturally without any breeding efforts and produce perfectly fertile hybrids. Today we know that wild einkorn is one of two ancestors of wild emmer. This natural hybrid was further developed through breeding into domesticated emmer and durum wheat. The second ancestor of emmer is unknown. Further hybridization of emmer with a closely related wild grass resulted in the formation of common wheat and spelt.

We know from archeological finds in the Fertile Crescent (p. 29) that all steps of hybridization were already being used as crops in the seventh millennium BC. Hybridization gave wheat its good growth characteristics under different soil and climatic conditions. An equally significant result of hybridization was a substantially greater yield than could be attained with the unmodified or cultivated ancestors.

In addition to high yield and adaptation to the respective environs, the goal of improving the processing quality of wheat became increasingly important to breeders. The actual breeding target of wheat and other cereals is the fruit (kernel), even though all parts of the plant above ground may be used as fodder.

With today's cereal crops the kernel mainly consists of the starch-containing endosperm. The natural function of the endosperm is to provide nutrition for the embryo (or germ, the part of the fruit most important for reproduction) from the time the seed germinates until photosynthesis begins in the green parts of the seedling. In the course of domestication the endosperm was increasingly focused upon by breeders so that kernels now contain about 70% starch. The protein content is approximately 12% of the total, and many minerals and vitamins are included as well.

In this context I would like to emphasize once again that the formation of such a large endosperm as a result of breeding is abnormal and greatly hinders reproduction of the plant in natural conditions. This corresponds closely with those plants illustrated in Figs. 16 and 17 (color plates II and III), where large harvests also demand extreme metabolic capacities of those organs which serve to provide nutrition. Analogous goals are pursued in many cases of animal breeding, e.g. with dairy cows.

In addition to yield and various other characteristics, the grinding efficiency of the kernels and the suitability of the flour for baking are also important in breeding common wheat. Modern kitchens and bakeries are geared to technical perfection and the rationalization of work. They require standardized flour so that every bag of a particular kind of flour will guarantee the desired type of bread, roll, or cake in exactly the same shape and size under precisely defined baking conditions. This calls for a standardized grinding process and a final flour quality that is as constant as possible. If necessary, flour products are therefore blended until the ash mass, the criterion for labeling flour varieties, equals a precise preset value.

The ash mass is a simple measure of the mineral content, which is in turn dependent on the degree of fineness to which the flour is ground. The commonly used wheat flour 405 (German flour type number) has, for example, 0.405% ash. Darker flour with a lesser degree of fineness and a higher content of nutritionally valuable components thus has a higher type number.

Figure 21 Comparison of the sizes of ears from wheat (left), triticale (center), and rye (right)

Triticale: An Extreme Case of Hybridization

The possibilities of hybridization have not yet been exhausted with common wheat and spelt. As early as the 19th century some species of wheat were found to spontaneously form additional hybrids, even with rye. From a breeding point of view the most interesting varieties are created when wheat (Triticum) is used as the female hybridization partner and rye (Secale) is used as the male. The result is a new crop, triticale, which was named by combining the Latin names of the parents.

Increasing interest in the agricultural use of triticale is based on several characteristics of resistance that the rye has contributed, as even with good varieties of wheat this has always been a weakness. Compared to wheat, triticale generally has increased hardiness, and like rye grows under less favorable climatic and soil conditions. Triticale is also less demanding than wheat with regard to irrigation.

According to the results of breeding tests the yield per hectare was not always as high as that of wheat, but in individual cases at least as high, and considerably higher than that of rye. A comparison of the size of the ears of triticale, wheat, and rye in Fig. 21 could give rise to an optimistic appraisal of further breeding attempts. Triticale already plays an important role as grain feed in temperate zones and in subtropical regions it is increasingly replacing wheat as a source of food for humans.

Weeds Become Crops: Oats and Rye

Oats and rye may be old crops in comparison with triticale, but they are newcomers compared to wheat and barley. Oats and rye are "secondary crops," and for a long time were primarily viewed as weeds (weed grasses) that were difficult to eradicate in stands of wheat and barley. During the deterioration of the climate in Central Europe in the first millennium BC. they proved to be especially hardy in comparison to wheat and barley. Together with millet they temporarily became some of the most important food plants in the damp and cool climatic zones of Europe.

Both oats and rye are of great nutritional value. And yet both of these cereals are now primarily used as cattle feed and each accounts for less than a tenth of the world's total wheat production. Their comparatively rapid development from weeds to crops of varying importance reveals the relativity of their value under different environmental or political conditions – right up to governmental policies that presently use a fixed price system for wheat and barley to suppress the cultivation of other cereal crops.

Special Features of Corn, Rapeseed and Sugar Beet

The diversity of breeding goals and products, as well as methodological approaches, is as wide as the food plants themselves. Three additional examples will be briefly examined. They may serve as representatives of many others before I conclude this overview with a look at another special case: the potato. These three examples stand for particularly successful improvements in yield (corn), nutritional quality (rapeseed), and farming technology (sugar beet). At the same time they illustrate the degree to which species-specific traits have to be taken into consideration.

Corn is the classic case for the practical application of *hybrid breeding*: the crossing of two different inbred lines from the same species. The results are hybrids with especially high yields and a favorable combination of characteristics on the part of the crossing partners. For unknown reasons, however, these high yields only occur in the first generation. The breeding of inbred parental lines thus has to be repeated each year. In order to inhibit self-fertilization a line either has to be "male-sterile" or has to be castrated by cutting off the male flowers. In practice the utilization of male sterility is a much easier method. This can be accomplished through breeding, based on natural mutations, and functions with corn as well as with several other plants.

The especially high yields achieved by the crossing of inbred lines occur in many plants, and this method is increasingly used in the cultivation of, for example, corn, rice, sugar beets, sorghum, and sunflowers. The hybrid seed, however, is expensive because it has to be created over and over again through corresponding crossings. It is nevertheless economically attractive and extensively used as an exceptionally high-yielding variety.

Rapeseed is the second case of a crop with special features, but here we are less concerned with the amount of yield as we are with the use of breeding to remove undesirable traits. Rapeseed is one of the most important oil plants and its importance is increasing around the world. In its original form rapeseed oil contains an uncommon fatty acid (erucic acid) which is absent in other vegetable oils produced from, for example, soybeans, peanuts, or sunflowers. The total share of this type of fatty acid can amount to 50% thus rapeseed oil was long considered to be of inferior quality as an edible oil. In the past it was generally used as lamp oil and by the paint and detergent industries.

Erucic acid-free varieties of rapeseed have now been bred ("o-varieties") and have proven to be high-quality edible oils. However, this amounted to the removal of only one of two undesirable types of ingredients.

Pressing the oil leaves remnants (press cake, rapeseed meal) which contain large amounts of protein and are highly valued as fodder. Until recently the quality of this fodder was greatly impaired by high concentrations of a toxic and unpalatable ingredient known as "mustard oil" (glucosinolate). Chemically related glucosinolates are found in all Brassicaceae species (cabbage, radish, mustard, etc.) and determine their characteristic taste. This problem was also solved through extensive breeding efforts. The final results are "oo-varieties" which yield oil nearly free of erucic acid and contain greatly reduced amounts of glucosinolates in the rapeseed meal.

Breeders of *sugar beets* faced a completely different type of challenge. Sugar beets originated from the Mediterranean area, were long a garden plant, and later served as a feed plant before becoming a source of sugar at the end of the 17th century. Due to systematic breeding their sugar content has grown from 7 to 23%.

Until recently the cultivation of sugar beets has been very labor- and cost-intensive because young plants had to be thinned out by hand. The reason for this particularity lay in the morphology of the flowers, which are normally combined in clusters of two to four sessile (stalk-less) blossoms. The developing seed clusters contain a corresponding number of ovules. Breeders succeeded in reducing them to one, making the seed *monogerm* (one-seeded) and thinning unnecessary.

Modern monogerm seed is produced in the form of pellets with pesticides in the coating, thus allowing these chemicals to be used sparingly and in a more environmentally compatible fashion.

The Potato as an Example

In this chapter the potato serves as the last example of the wide range of breeding goals. The potato tuber is the world's most important food source after the prevailing types of cereal (wheat, rice, and corn). Its geographic origin is the Andes area of South America. Potatoes already served as a main source of nutrition for early advanced Native American cultures (Moche, Nazca) more than 2000 years ago and had been domesticated several thousand years earlier.

Toward the end of the 16th century Spanish conquerors brought a South American potato cultivar to Europe. Soon afterwards, during the Thirty Years' War, potatoes were sporadically cultivated and at the same time spread across Europe to North America. However, their importance as a staple food in the Northern Hemisphere was not recognized for some time. In the beginning it was misjudged completely. It was not only used as an ornamental plant in gardens, but in giving it a name people also

Figure 22 Comparison of the sizes of tubers from a wild type and a modern high-yielding variety of potato

mistook the tubers for the fruiting body of truffles: In Germany potatoes, which are now known as *Kartoffeln*, were originally called *Tartüffel* (from the Italian word *tartufo* = truffle).

Frederick the Great is credited with finally pushing through the acceptance of the potato in Central Europe. However, he allegedly needed an unusual method to convince farmers of the new crop's advantages. As the story goes, the king made them curious by placing soldiers around a field during daylight hours. As expected, at night farmers stole the obviously valuable potatoes and planted them themselves. His success can be measured by the fact that a scant few decades later (1845–48) severe famines were caused by failed potato harvests in parts of Europe.

In the meantime, approximately 200 years of intensive breeding have produced a nearly indeterminate assortment of potato varieties. Tuber size and quantity of yield have dramatically increased compared to the original wild types (Fig. 22). In addition – as with every crop – there have been numerous general breeding goals as well as species- and user-specific features.

The general goals are typical: the greatest possible tolerance of different climatic and soil conditions, disease resistance, uniform maturity, a long shelf life, etc. Taste, cooking behavior, color, form, and usability for mechanical processing (French fries, chips, mashed potato powder, dumpling flour, peeled canned potatoes, starch, and alcohol) are particularly specific to the potato and the different ways in which its tuber is used.

In order to appreciate the breadth of demands placed on the breeding of potatoes, one only needs to take a look at some of the different customary requirements. German cuisine prefers yellow potatoes, Anglo-Saxon white; chips should have a uniform diameter and no dark spots; French fries should be as long as possible; canned potatoes as small as possible (and they should not turn brown when stored); fresh potatoes should have a high protein content, and those used for starch and alcohol production should contain as much starch as possible.

For farming, the propagation of potatoes is mainly vegatative (asexual) and involves the use of tubers, whereas breeding requires sexual reproduction and the growing of young plants from seed. The possibility of vegetative propagation is a special feature of plants, as opposed to animals. The potato is among those plants that are particularly easy to propagate vegetatively, not only through the use of tubers or cuttings, but even from small pieces of tissue or single cells.

This form of regenerating entire plants from a few or even one *somatic cell*, or body cell (as opposed to *gametes* or *germ cells*) has become an important tool in plant breeding, including plant genetic engineering. A short look at the possibilities of tissue and cell culture will thus bring this chapter to a close.

Tissue and Cell Culture

Knowledge about tissue and cell culture has existed in plant research for 100 years. This knowledge has been further developed into an extensive field of research and has led to many practical applications. In many plant breeding companies they are now routinely used for the generation and propogation of seedlings (Fig. 23, color plate IV).

The cultivation of cells from higher, multicellular organisms outside their natural tissues has been practiced for some time now with plant, animal, and human cells. In medical and pharmaceutical research it is often applied, for example, to avoid experiments with living organisms. In the case of humans and animals, the cells or pieces of tissue can be taken from the skin, muscle, bone marrow, liver, kidney, and other organs, and in the case of plants likewise from many different types of tissue.

In suitable nutrient solutions the cells often divide for long periods of time. Human and most animal cells, however, can no longer substantially change the program of specialization in their natural cellular environment. Damaged tissue can indeed be replenished through cell division, for instance in the healing process of skin, bones, muscle, or tendons, but a bone cell does not turn into a skin cell, and vice versa.

This is the major difference between plants and animals. A simple example is the propagation of plants with cuttings. A branch that has been cut off and put into the soil does not contain a single root cell. And yet, the different types of specialized cells in this branch are able to form roots through division and simultaneous reprogramming within a short period of time. These roots are no different than those formed during normal development from seed.

Fig. 24 (color plate V) shows a comparison of these different potentials in plant and animal cell cultures. The potato is used as a typical example on the plant side. A small piece of tissue from an organ (leaf, stem, root, tuber, etc.) is dipped into a disinfectant to prevent microbial contamination and then placed into a liquid or onto a solid nutrient medium. This contains a source of carbon, e.g. sugar, all the necessary minerals, and a few vitamins and plant-specific growth regulators.

The tissue then grows into an undifferentiated cell mass (callus), similar to the healing of a wound on an intact plant (as in a callus on the stub of a branch that has been cut off). By shaking the callus in a liquid nutrient solution the mass breaks into small fragments and single cells that will continue to divide indefinitely if a regular supply of nutrients is provided.

Plant cells exhibit another special feature as well: They are surrounded by a rigid cell wall that can be broken down by some specialized microorganisms. The responsible enzymes can be easily isolated, allowing for the production of otherwise undamaged, wall-less cells that are only surrounded by a membrane. These *protoplasts* are valuable interim stages for genetic modifications and will therefore play an important role in the next chapter.

The regeneration of intact plants from single cells, or from small or large calluses or pieces of tissue, is effected through step by step changes in the composition of plant growth regulators in the nutrient medium. The reprogramming of cells caused by this kind of sequential treatment first causes the formation of shoots and then roots (Fig. 24, color plate V). The plant thus created can be planted in the soil just like any rooted cutting or a seedling generated through sexual propagation. Because they all descend from the same plant, they are genetically identical clones, just like grafts, runners, or cuttings would be.

The potential for plant propagation becomes clearer when one considers that a single leaf consists of millions of cells. Valuable individuals can be propagated in nearly unlimited numbers from protoplasts (e.g. variants with new, rare, or especially distinct types of resistance; plants free of viruses or microbial pathogens that are otherwise difficult to control).

Nevertheless, it should be borne in mind that all individuals that descend from the same plant represent, as genetically identical clones, an extreme case of inbreeding. They lack the natural range of genetic diversity, which has to be restored if required.

One field of application with great potential for employing cell and tissue culture is genetic engineering. The following chapter is thus dedicated to this topic.

Summary

The breeding of food plants aims at the creation of cultivars that yield the greatest possible amounts of high-quality food under particular environmental and agricultural conditions. This goal has been followed for approximately 10,000 years; at first with the use of "blind" breeding by selection, and for the past 100 years by combining selection with specifically target-oriented, science-based cross-breeding. More recently, cross-breeding has been complemented by the chemical or physical triggering of mutations, as well as tissue and cell culture technology.

The original forms of our most important food plants were domesticated in or near "biodiversity centers" (regions with a particularly large genetic diversity). From there they were disseminated around the world by way of trade, colonization, and adaptation due to breeding. Modern high-yielding varieties differ significantly from their original wild types both in outward appearance (phenotype) and in their genetic constitution (genotype). They would never have existed at all if breeders had not forced their evolution in the intended direction. They are usually much less competitive in nature than the wild types and therefore require intensive mechanical and chemical protection.

5 Genetic Engineering in Research and Application

At the end of the 20th century genetic engineering ushered in a new era in plant breeding and in many other areas of biological research and application. Genetic engineering now plays such an important role in human health and in agriculture that a brief outline of the method and of some initial achievements may be helpful as a prerequisite for further discussions.

Genetic Engineering: A New Branch of Biotechnology

Genetic engineering is the practical application of methods that molecular biology, a very young branch of the biological sciences, has developed over the past few decades. This new course of research and its methodological basis have an unusual history. Its origin lies, apart from notable contributions of theoretical physicists, in the overlap of several specific fields of biology which long appeared as strictly separate disciplines: biochemistry, microbiology, cell biology, and genetics.

No other branch of biology has developed so vehemently with as many consequences as molecular biology – not least of all because, after a brief period of independence, it once again merged with its source disciplines and fundamentally revolutionized them by serving as a scientific link and by providing methodological tools of unexpected efficiency.

The genetic engineering that developed from this new type of research is the youngest scion of an ancient technology, i.e. biotechnology, which deals with the practical application of biological processes. For many thousands of years, for instance, lactic bacteria, yeast, and other microorganisms have been specially bred in order to convert milk into cheese, to bake bread, and to produce beer and wine through alcohol fermentation. In modern medicine specially bred microorganisms represent the key sources of a continuously growing number of antibiotics and other pharmaceuticals.

In a comprehensive sense of the term, all of these processes are "genetic engineering," i.e. the breeding or goal-oriented genetic modification (optimization) of organisms for biotechnological purposes.

Inheritance from a Bio-molecular Perspective

The genes of every organism – from the smallest bacteria to the largest redwood tree or elephant, right up to highly bred wheat cultivars or to humans – are all made of the same four basic elements, or nucleotides. Every gene contains several thousand of these nucleotides strung together in different sequences that are unique to each individual gene. With a length of 1000 elements (most genes are substantially longer) there is already an unimaginable number of possible combinations (4^{1000}) of these four basic building blocks. With this in mind, it is easy to deduce that with great probability every existing sequence will never occur more than once in the whole universe, thus making every gene – and even more so, every organism – absolutely unique.

Within each cell the genes are connected to each other in long chains. Together, packed in tight bundles, they form the

genome, an organism's complete package of genetic information. A perfect copy of the genome is made when a cell divides
and this information is inherited by each new cell (with multiple repetitions for all following cells). One rare but important
qualification is that a few errors in copying can have far-reaching
consequences (pp. 101ff).

Every cell of an individual (with rare exceptions that are
without relevance here) contains exactly the same complete
genetic information. Through a sophisticated mechanism this
information is translated into proteins, each one of which has a
special function in the cell. Most of the proteins serve as building
blocks for the cell's structure or as catalytically active enzymes
(molecular "skilled laborers" in cell metabolism). Every enzyme,
as a specific catalyst (reaction accelerator), is responsible for a
particular metabolic function, e.g. for one step in the formation
of a flower pigment, of starch in the endosperm of a kernel of
grain, of new copies of genes in cell division, etc.

The intensities with which the many different metabolic activities proceed are dependent on the functional specialization of
the cells in the different types of tissue, on the age and developmental stage of the organism, and on the external conditions
(light, temperature, and the supply of nutrients and water). The
number and thus the overall activity of the respective enzyme
molecules changes accordingly. The detailed regulatory control
of the translation of genes into proteins is provided by the
dichotomy of the gene structure. In addition to a segment that
contains the instructions for the encoded protein (the structural
gene) every gene also has a control unit (the promoter) that regis-
ters all the incoming signals in the cell's nucleus, thus regulating
the gene's activity.

Considering the overall metabolic complexity within cells or
entire organisms, this form of data processing consists of what

is still an incalculable diversity and multitude of combinatorial permutations of signaling molecules, promoter structures, and regulatory circuits that orchestrate a highly sophisticated, multifaceted interplay of effect and counter effect.

At present, there is probably no biological field of research that is being worked on as intensively as this one – the very basis of life. All the results thus far have confirmed the long-cherished supposition that the entire multiplicity, complexity, dynamism, variability, and plasticity of biological systems are reflected at this molecular level.

And yet, the more we attempt to discover about the molecular mechanisms of regulation, the clearer it becomes that there are as many detailed answers as there are genes, cell types, and cellular states. Therefore, perhaps the most important knowledge that molecular biology has generated for basic research and the practice of genetic engineering is the conclusion indicated at the outset:

> The "genetic code" (the chemical nature of the four building blocks of the genes and the encoded information) universally applies to all organisms, from the simplest bacteria to humans.

Further along in this chapter several examples will show what far-reaching consequences this "universality of the genetic code" has had for the practice of genetic engineering. Prior to this, however, a short overview of the methodological tools will help explain the practical procedures.

The Technology of Gene Transfer

While with sexual propagation half of all the thousands of largely unidentified genes from each crossing partner are mixed together in a unique random combination, genetic engineering transfers one or a few individual genes with known functions. The most important steps are schematically illustrated in Fig. 25 (color plate VI).

At first the genetic material (the DNA = deoxyribonucleic acid) is isolated from an organism possessing a desired gene. Dissecting the long chains into individual gene segments (DNA fragments) is achieved with the help of *restriction enzymes*. These molecular cutting devices identify certain nucleotide sequences with high specificity and split the chains at these recognition sites.

Restriction enzymes were originally discovered in bacteria as a natural mechanism for preventing the penetration of foreign DNA (from viruses, for example) and are now commercially produced in large numbers. With their help any gene can be cut out of a particular section of the genome and, if required, dissected into its two functional parts, structural gene and promoter.

The second step (right in Fig. 25, color plate VI) involves the linking of the structural gene with a suitable promoter, which will regulate the desired expression of the newly composed gene in the target organism under the appropriate conditions. Examples of highly specific expressions of foreign genes in *transgenic* plants are pathogen infection sites (p. 158) or areas damaged by insect bites (p. 135).

In the last step the prepared gene is transferred into the target cell or organism. There are several techniques for achieving this in plants. The simplest method is the direct addition of DNA to a protoplast suspension. Under suitable conditions of cultivation, most cell types will willingly accept the additional DNA.

An important discovery was made at a very early stage in the development of these methods. It was crucial for the further establishment of genetic engineering and had to do with the fate of the genes which had been transferred and with their new environment. It was discovered that different types of foreign genes were not only accepted by a target cell, but could also be stably integrated in its genome. They could thus be inherited and the genetic modification would be preserved for generations.

In order to complete this picture, however, it should be noted that the integration, expression, and inheritability of such a *transgene* only occurs with a certain statistical probability and that the "stable" integration is not necessarily of infinite duration. And yet, more remarkable than this limitation is the phenomenon itself: it proves that individual genes or sections of genes can be incorporated into an existing genome, can exercise their original function in a new biological environment, and can be inherited by succeeding generations.

Another observation was equally important: If the new gene has a promoter of foreign origin, it will be expressed in the target organism in the same way as an indigenous gene with its own, functionally analogous promoter.

The upper part of Fig. 25 (color plate VI) and its continuation in Fig. 24 (color plate V) illustrate the subsequent steps to a complete plant. A genotype altered in this way contains only one or a few additional transgenes, and remains otherwise unchanged.

Crucial to the successful completion of this multistage procedure is the possibility, if required, of multiplying the DNA as much as needed at each stage in specially constructed laboratory strains of the intestinal bacteria Escherichia coli (E. coli). Bacterial mutants which are only able to survive under artificial conditions are used for this replication step, so that their uncontrolled spread outside of the laboratory is ruled out with a high degree of certainty.

Without going into greater detail, I would like to add at this stage that there is also the possibility of deactivating individual genes through genetic engineering. A well-known example of this alternative option was the genetically modified tomato variety "FlavorSavor," where a few years ago a decaying of the fruit was considerably delayed through the deactivation of one of the genes involved. These tomatoes no longer had to be harvested before ripening, as is usually practiced, and did not have to be artificially ripened by chemical treatment before delivery. They were able to develop their full taste and nutrient content naturally, without decaying soon thereafter.

On the whole, the possibilities of molecular biology and genetic engineering have completely revolutionized our knowledge of biology within a few decades, similar to the way Max Planck, Albert Einstein and others revolutionized our physical image of the world nearly a century earlier. In each case the scientific revolution was based on a series of unexpected results which led to unforeseen practical applications.

Instead of an extensive list, a few selected examples should illustrate some early cases of the practical application of genetic engineering.

Genetic Engineering with Bacteria

Bacteria served as model organisms in the initial development of genetic engineering as well as in the first practical tests. They were not only the first and relatively easily accessible objects of basic research; from the very beginning they also served as an essential aid in the replication of DNA.

The practical application either involves the modification (intensification, removal, or alteration) of an existing genetically determined trait, or the formation of a new product that would normally not be generated by the organism in question. While modifications are commonly also achievable with conventional breeding methods, the formation of a product which is foreign to the species, with the exception of a few special cases, is only possible using genetic engineering. In principle the approach is the same as with the transfer of genes to plant protoplasts (Fig. 25, color plate VI).

One of the first and therefore especially well-known examples is the genetically engineered production of human insulin in transgenic bacteria. Insulin is a pancreatic hormone that plays an important role in the regulation of the blood sugar level in higher animals and humans. A deficiency of insulin leads to diabetes, a widespread and often inherited disease whose frequency is steadily increasing, especially as adult-onset diabetes. The only possible therapy is a strict diet combined with regular injections of insulin.

In view of the millions of patients, however, the small quantities of human insulin that previously had to be isolated from the pancreata of the deceased was completely inadequate. Although insulin from pigs was used as a substitute, it is not completely identical to human insulin in its chemical composition and therefore not free of side effects. On the other hand, the chemical synthesis of human insulin is very complicated and expensive, and the complete and cost-effective separation of by-products is practically impossible.

Human insulin is a very small protein and was therefore ideally suited for the development of a method yielding a medically valuable product by genetic engineering. The result was a milestone in the history of this new method: In 1979 the production of human insulin in E. coli was published by a genetic engineering company founded in the United States three years before. In 1983 the product was brought onto the market by an established pharmaceutical company under the name Humulin as the first genetically engineered medicament.

Humulin is identical to human insulin in both chemical structure and clinical effect. After further improvement this method is now being safely und routinely applied to the production of great quantities worldwide. However, public and political acceptance was lagging considerably behind in many countries. Although the demand in Germany, for example, was great, and a facility for genetically engineered production was built already in the 1980s, the responsible state government at the time prohibited its application. In doing so they set a signal for the long-term relocation of pharmaceutical research and production involved with genetic engineering to other countries. This had corresponding consequences for jobs and tax revenues in an industrial sector in which Germany had been a worldwide leader up to that point. At the same time, the domestic demand for insulin was covered by the legal importation of the genetically engineered product from abroad!

In the meantime, more and more valuable substances for medical and other uses, including large-scale industrial purposes, are being produced in bacteria using genetic engineering. For the subsequent discussion in Chapters 7 and 9 two conclusions based on experience to date are important:

- The spread of genetically modified organisms with potentially disadvantageous effects for humans or the environment has been effectively prevented by the exclusive use of bacterial strains which are dependent on special laboratory conditions.

- Numerous hormones, growth factors, blood clotting factors, and other lifesaving medicaments that are otherwise unavailable or difficult to access were made available by this method for the first time.

Medical Research

Genetically engineered modifications have opened up many new fields of application, for instance with higher unicellular organisms (yeasts, etc.) or with plant, animal or human cells in suspension culture. In medical research animal and human cell cultures have become irreplaceable aids. In addition, the identification of genetic functions in several well-investigated model organisms (fruit flies, zebra fish, mice, and rats) is becoming increasingly important for research into the causes and treatments of human diseases.

Results thus far open up a broad spectrum of valuable potential uses for genetic engineering:

- The application of genetic engineering signifies a great qualitative leap in the investigation of the causes and possible treatments of diseases.
- Viral diseases (including AIDS) that are based on the transfer and spread of viral genetic information in human bodies can only be sensibly investigated with molecular biological or genetic engineering methods. The same applies to all types of cancer where a malfunctioning of genes causes the development and spread of tumors.
- The majority of human illnesses and diseases can still not be treated effectively. Despite intensive research, the specific causes are either not or at best insufficiently known. Among these are widespread diseases which often exhibit

extremely complicated symptoms, such as influenza, rheumatism, arthritis, cancer, AIDS, Alzheimer's disease, and arteriosclerosis (heart and circulatory diseases). There are also many less common, but not less serious cases of genetically inherited or infectious diseases.

- A specific and effective therapy that is virtually free of side effects is only possible with a precise knowledge of the causes of a disease. Basic research is the absolute prerequisite for a practical curative approach.

- The number of organisms, including humans, whose genome has been deciphered either in part or as a whole is increasing rapidly. Comparing the results with one another as well as in conjunction with human genetics and disease research in laboratory animals, e.g. cancer in mice, has created a completely new basis for the molecular understanding of these diseases and the treatments derived from this knowledge. In particular, the fundamentals of many inherited human diseases would simply not be accessible with other methods.

Genetic Engineering in Plant Breeding

In addition to basic biological and medical research, and the manufacturing of pharmaceuticals and other valuable products, plant breeding is the third large field of application for genetic engineering. For several years gene technology-assisted plant breeding ("plant genetic engineering,") has become increasingly important in the development of a type of agriculture that is not only efficient, but considerate of the environment at the same time. Numerous examples in the following passages and the next chapter will provide evidence of this potential.

The first commercially applied breeding results which would not have been accessible without genetic engineering are particular forms of insect resistance and herbicide tolerance. Both of these traits were achieved by transferring bacterial genes to plants. The transgenic varieties thus created have been used for some years, especially in the United States, Canada, Brazil, Argentina and China, and are being cultivated in rapidly increasing amounts (p. 20).

Insect Resistance

The bacterium Bacillus thuringiensis (Bt) has the noteworthy feature of being able to excrete a protein that is highly toxic to certain insect pests. This protein has been given the shortened name of the bacterium and is called Bt-toxin. Due to its selective toxicity, which is limited to a few species of insects, the bacterium has been used in agriculture within the scope of large-scale biological pest control spraying programs.

Bt-toxin is a very large protein, but even about half of it retains full toxicity. The responsible bacterial gene was accordingly shortened, combined with a suitable plant promoter, as shown in Fig. 25 (color plate VI), and transferred to plants which then expressed the trait wherever insects attacked.

This procedure was applied to several major crop plants, including corn and cotton which respectively underwent severe attack by corn borers and bollworms before this form of protection was introduced. After egg deposition the hatched insect larvae develop within the plant's stalks, feeding there and causing great damage, which is seriously aggravated by fungal infections and the formation of particularly strong fungal toxins.

The interior of the plant's stalk is not readily accessible to

Figure 26 Comparison of a control plant (left) with a Bt-toxin producing
          transgenic tobacco plant (right) after an insect infestation

conventional pesticides. By contrast, in transgenic plants the Bt-
toxin forms directly where the plant is attacked, thus preventing
any further development of pests and fungal toxins. Fig. 26 illustrates the effectiveness, using a test object as an example.

Before this indirect form of biological pest control was commercially used in agriculture several variations of the Bt-toxin
had been tested with regard to their compatibility with useful
insects. All of those variants now in use were found to be toxi-
cologically safe.

In the meantime Bt crops have been cultivated in numerous
industrial and developing countries. According to an investigation by Clive James (*Preview: Global Status of Commercialized
Biotech/GM Crops*), by 2004 two-thirds of all cotton fields in
China, one of the world's main areas of cultivation, had already
been planted with transgenic Bt cotton plants. In South Africa

this figure was even as high as 85%. In his most recent status report from the year 2007, Clive James documents further substantial increases in Bt cotton cultivation, particularly in India and China.

In an analysis by Matin Qaim and Ira Matuschke (*Impacts of genetically modified crops in developing countries: a survey*), the authors considered the ancillary question of how much the cultivation of transgenic cotton plants actually benefited developing countries and the environment. Concrete data was compiled for Argentina, China, Mexico, and South Africa. According to their results, the application of insecticides with the use of Bt cotton was reduced on average by 50% (from 33% in South Africa to 77% in Mexico) and the average yields grew by 20%. Despite higher prices for seed, users were thereby able to earn considerable profits, which ranged from 18 US dollars per hectare in South Africa to 470 US dollars in China. The share of the farmers' profits in comparison with seed manufacturers fluctuated between 21% in Argentina and 94% in China. The average value for all five countries was 65%. Remarkably (see Chapter 8), small farmers' profits were even greater than those of medium-sized and large operations.

Because cotton farming requires the use of more pesticides than any other major crop worldwide, the environment profits greatly as well – not to mention the positive effects on the health of farmers and agricultural laborers who often do not know how to properly employ protective measures when applying pesticides.

Herbicide Tolerance

Herbicide tolerance can be achieved in different ways. We have seen that herbicides are synthetic agents which in particular concentrations are tolerated by some crops while being toxic to weeds (p. 78). Varying sensitivity to herbicides is based on typal differences in the fine structure of plant proteins attacked by the herbicides. By definition herbicides are toxic for plants (Latin *herba* = plant, weed) but not for other organisms. This is because of proteins that are only found in plants and are, for instance, involved with photosynthesis or with the absorption, transport or detoxification of the herbicide through plant-specific mechanisms. Using genetic engineering methods, breeding is specifically targeted at these reactions, for example through the transfer of

- an additional copy of the gene encoding the herbicide-sensitive protein which is then produced in large amounts, thus diluting the herbicide's effects;
- a plant gene that has been modified using genetic engineering and now encodes a protein with a different fine structure and reduced sensitivity to herbicides;
- a gene from microorganisms that causes a similar effect;
- a gene from microorganisms that produces an enzyme which was not originally present in transgenic plants and converts the herbicide into an ineffective compound.

Fig. 27 illustrates a typical result. Once again, this involved a pilot project which was then applied to different crops and finally, after the usual extensive testing and official certification procedures, led to marketable varieties.

More than three-quarters of the transgenic plants cultivated around the world are herbicide-tolerant soybean, rapeseed, corn, and cotton varieties. Of these, soybean currently exhibits the largest share of all genetically engineered plants. The financial advantages of cultivating transgenic herbicide-tolerant plants

Figure 27 Herbicide tolerance of a genetically engineered rapeseed plant
(left) in comparison with an unaltered control plant (right)

may be substantially less than with Bt cotton, but through the
use of herbicides that are safer for the environment the ecological
profits are great as well.

An additional transgenic plant species that has proved itself
over several years of commercial use is virus-resistant papaya.
It will serve as an example of the successful application of a
new resistance mechanism for plant viruses in the next chapter
(pp. 159ff.).

Diagnostics

In modern plant breeding the identification of hereditary traits at intermediate breeding stages or in new varieties has been vastly improved by the application of the novel tool of molecular diagnostics. Up to now, after every crossing step, individuals with the desired characteristics in the proper combination and intensity had to be selected from the entire population through an elaborate evaluation procedure and thoroughly tested before the next step. It is easy to imagine just how much effort is required, for example, to simultaneously follow two or more traits that are difficult to even test individually (e.g. applying and analyzing infections for disease resistance as well as frost periods for winter hardiness).

Molecular diagnosis through "DNA-marker technology" provides for substantial simplification. It allows for verification of genetically identified traits with simple molecular biological methods in a laboratory. The technology uses DNA or gene fragments which, due to their high degree of specificity (p. 125), unequivocally locate individuals with the desired gene or gene combination.

This technology is now an established and methodologically well-developed routine procedure in plant breeding. However, unambiguous DNA markers are thus far only available for a limited number of breeding goals as definite proof of causal relationships between individual traits and the responsible genes has only been established in a few cases. Nevertheless, in view of the fact that this new method of trait recognition makes work much easier and cost-effective, rapid progress in this field of gene technology may be expected.

Summary

Genetic engineering is the practical application of molecular biology. In contrast to conventional breeding by crossing and selection, where genes can only be indirectly recognized through observable heritable traits, genetic engineering uses individual genes with known molecular functions. In principle, every gene can be transferred to every organism. The gene has to have a species-appropriate regulatory unit (promoter) that specifically regulates its expression through the perception of signals from the respective cellular environment.

Plants containing genetically engineered hereditary information can – in contrast to animals – be created from almost every type of tissue (leaf, stem, root, etc.), e.g. through the cultivation of somatic (asexual) cells. The appropriate choice of the promoter, which can be derived from any other gene, will assure that the foreign gene in the transgenic plant will be expressed according to the specificity of this regulatory unit.

The greatest progress in the commercial use of genetic engineering has been made with bacteria. Genetic engineering procedures have also proven their great potential in basic biological and medical research, in the production of pharmaceuticals, as well as in the breeding of plants.

In comparison with conventional breeding the most important innovations of genetic engineering include: (1) the transfer of one or more genes that may or may not be foreign to a species and would not be acquired through sexual crossing; (2) the free combination of promoters and structural genes to achieve the desired cellular expression of a trait; (3) the selective deactivation or removal of individual genes; and (4) the alteration of particular sections of genes in order to specifically modify a trait.

Figure 2 Aerial view of a Central European cultivated landscape

Figure 16 Five species of the Solanaceae family, each of which has one of four different organs particularly emphasized by breeders: the petunia's flowers, the tobacco plant's leaves, the pepper and tomato plants' fruit, and the potato's tuber

Figure 17 Five common species of the Brassicaceae family, in which, similar to Figure 16 (color plate II), different organs were particularly emphasized by breeders: the cauliflower's inflorescence, rapeseed's oleiferous seeds, cabbage's leaves, kohlrabi's swollen stem, and rutabaga's (yellow turnip) main root

Figure 23 Propagation of plants (in this case sugar beets) from cultured cells in a plant breeding company: callus cultures are sequentially treated with appropriate plant growth regulators to first form shoots (upper left), and then roots (upper right)

The seedlings are transferred to greenhouses until ready for planting outdoors

Figure 24 The ability of single cells or pieces of tissue to regenerate into complete plants that are genetically identical to the source plant (clones)

Human and most animal somatic cells do not have this ability

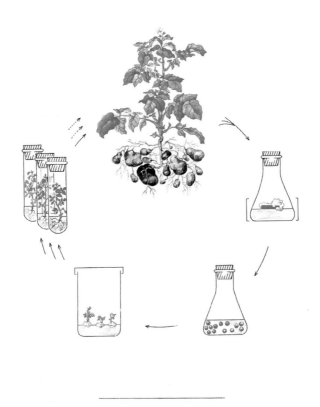

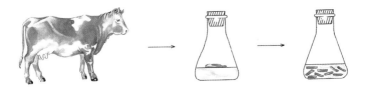

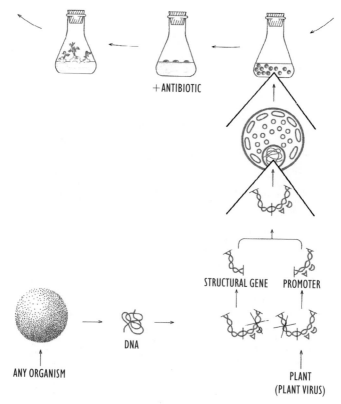

+ANTIBIOTIC

STRUCTURAL GENE   PROMOTER

DNA

ANY ORGANISM

PLANT
(PLANT VIRUS)

Figure 25 Schematic illustration of the transfer of individual genes to
plant cells and their subsequent regeneration into intact plants.
In this example unchanged cells are killed with an antibiotic
(p. 232) so that only transgenic plants are obtained

Figure 30 Field trial of transgenic potato plants destroyed by genetic
engineering opponents

Figure 28 Grains of rice with different contents of provitamin A: unaltered (white, upper left); 1.6 µg/g (yellow, lower left); 30 µg/g (yellow-orange, right)

Figure 29 Comparison of a transgenic (left) with a genetically unaltered potato plant (right) after treatment with the causal agent of potato blight

Figure 31 Comparison of transgenic virus-resistant papaya (right) with the corresponding unmodified control plants (left).

6 Old and New Breeding Goals

There are important reasons why breeders should continue to make great efforts to improve quality and yield, as well as to achieve the largest possible diversity of food and forage plants:

- the unabated growth of the human population;
- the limited availability of agricultural land and its simultaneous decrease due to urban and infrastructure development, as well as various other forms of land use or deterioration;
- the poor nutritional quality of some main food sources;
- environmental pollution caused by agriculture;
- the rapid adaptability of pests to frequently and extensively cultivated crops;
- the ecologically alarming decline of natural biodiversity and cultivar diversity in regions with intensive farming.

Genetic engineering has joined traditional methods of breeding as an innovative aid. The limits of its practical application are seldom the technology as such. Limiting factors are still primarily the number of functionally identified genes and knowledge about their regulatory mechanisms. This requires that intensive basic research be continued, particularly with regard to complex polygenic hereditary traits.

Just as in the field of medicine (p. 133), basic research and the application of results in plant breeding cannot be separated from one another. Essentially, no breeder will be able to do without a broad spectrum of fundamental knowledge. In most cases, however, the basic principles are developed by others. This corresponds to the traditional division of tasks between plant breeding companies and institutions that pursue pure basic research for the purpose of increasing scientific knowledge. The results of their research are essential prerequisites for methodological progress and new fields of application in breeding.

Thus a few examples of this interdependence that directly relate to the preceding chapter are presented. There we were able to see just how detailed our knowledge already is with regard to the structure and function of genes. However, in spite of these great achievements many basic issues about which we still know very little remain. Yet we can ask the next unanswered questions in such a specific way that they can now be approached with concrete research projects. For example:

How does a plant cell accommodate a foreign gene in its genome? Does integration occur in a particular or in a random position? Are the stability of integration, the inheritability, and the expression dependent on the position in the genome? How does a limited number of signaling molecules regulate thousands of different genes at the same time in a precisely coordinated manner? How does the respective fine-tuning allow for the various highly specialized functions of cells, tissues and organs, as well as the stage of development, the nutritional and the overall environmental conditions of the entire organism? How can a foreign promoter regulate the expression of a gene in a transgenic plant in exactly the same way as in the source plant, even though it does not occur with the same nucleotide sequence in the transgenic plant?

And, above all, the question for which there will presumably be as many answers as concrete, individual cases: Which genes are involved, and to what extent, with the polygenic hereditary traits so interesting for breeders, and which conditions have to be fulfilled for them to interact in an optimal fashion?

This is just a small selection of the many open questions, the answers to which would certainly be of great benefit to both breeding and scientific progress. As a new and powerful method, genetic engineering will continue to rapidly gain in importance – in contrast to a widespread fallacy, not as a substitute for but as a supplement to traditional breeding methods.

Genetic Engineering: Not a Substitute, Rather an Aid to Conventional Plant Breeding

Although plant genetic engineering has considerably broadened the spectrum of breeding possibilities, it cannot replace conventional plant breeding. The actual innovation, the transfer of individual genes that may even be foreign to the species, is only one of two complementary steps on the way to a new marketable variety. The initial product has to be further developed until all criteria required for licensing are fulfilled.

This second step will continue to be carried out by conventional breeding, regardless of whether the first step – the introduction or improvement of a desired trait – employed genetic engineering or not. All of the currently used transgenic cotton, corn, rapeseed, and soybean plants with genetically engineered insect resistance or herbicide tolerance (pp. 135ff.) were further developed to the point of licensing with traditional methods.

Conventional crossings will therefore continue to be a major part of the development of new varieties. In order to clarify the expected contributions of genetic engineering, I will nevertheless focus on such projects in the following examples where plant genetic engineering plays a significant role.

Before this, however, it is important to point out another indispensable, and yet often neglected, permanent task of conventional breeding.

Maintenance Breeding

In Europe, which is exceptionally favored by its climate and soils and therefore extremely prolific in the production of food, the question is often asked as to why we need plant breeding at all when we are already able to use existing high-yielding varieties to produce and destroy a surplus of food – a highly questionable practice in both financial and ecological terms.

Looked at from this viewpoint, the question seems justified. However, it fails to take account of the situation in many other parts of the world and ignores the basic biological fact that every combination of traits in a new variety will only remain in the initial form and intensity as long as selection pressure continues through breeding. For this reason every cultivar worth preserving must undergo *maintenance breeding* in order to prevent the loss of its distinctive characteristics – unless it already serves as a starting point for the development of a new variety with further improved or otherwise altered traits.

The reason for this necessity is the biological evolution that occurs unceasingly in all living organisms: the spontaneous mutations and new combinations of parental genes that take place with every step of sexual propagation. As soon as selection pressure decreases, the unavoidable consequence is a steady reduction in genetic purity due to a continuing loss of the cultivar-specific combination of traits.

Maintenance breeding is therefore an extensive field of activity for breeders. In its practical execution it corresponds to the above-mentioned second breeding step, and thus uses purely conventional breeding methods.

Food Quality

In the early phase of plant cultivation maintenance breeding was certainly not a conscious goal, but rather an unintentional side effect of selection. By contrast, quality improvement must have played a significant role right from the outset. Various types of illness must have resulted from nutrient deficiency and poisoning due to unbalanced diets of poorly developed crops.

Despite the many long-term breeding successes, even today's highly developed varieties of our main food plants do not contain sufficient quantities of all required nutritional elements. No less problematic are food allergies that have increasingly taken the place of direct (not caused by microorganisms) food poisoning.

The most important quality demands on our food and several common deficiency illnesses have already been mentioned (pp. 124ff.). The problem of allergies will be discussed below in a different context (p. 187). At this point a very special case of quality improvement should serve to indicate the limits of conventional breeding on the one hand, and the level to which plant genetic engineering has advanced on the other.

Rice is a staple food for approximately half of the world's population, and in favorable conditions it is supplemented with vegetables, fruit, meat, and fish to make a nutritionally well-balanced diet. These supplements are missing in part or as a whole, however, for hundreds of millions of poverty-stricken people in Asia, Africa, and Latin America. The results are severe signs of deficiency.

One of the most conspicuous signs of deficiency due to a one-sided or exclusive diet of rice is caused by the absence of provitamin A, a mixture of beta-carotene and chemically related precursors of vitamin A. The human body cannot produce these compounds by itself, but it can convert them to vitamin A.

In addition to various other functions, vitamin A is essential for the development and maintenance of eyesight and an intact immune system. A lack of provitamin A therefore leads to poor eyesight or even complete blindness and also weakens the immune defense, thus increasing the danger of infection. Small children, pregnant women, and nursing mothers are especially at risk. Because of vitamin A deficiency hundreds of thousands of preschool children go blind in developing countries each year. Half of them die within a year. It is estimated that from one to three million people die of malnutrition each year.

Similarly, for poor people in several Latin American and African countries corn or sweet potatoes are almost the sole sources of nutrition. However, particularly in the case of sweet potato, breeding efforts have yielded varieties with a sufficiently high content of provitamin A, small amounts of which had always been present.

Grains of rice, by contrast, do not even contain minute amounts of provitamin A that could be increased by conventional breeding. Genetic engineering offered the only possible solution via a transfer of suitable genes from bacteria or plants. The resulting transgenic rice varieties no longer produced provitamin A exclusively in the non-edible, green parts of the plant as they did before, but now in the grains as well. Because of the rice's new golden-yellow color the transgenic plant became known as "Golden Rice."

The breeding process itself as well as the many steps along the way to licensing the new variety provide interesting insight into the numerous challenges that plant genetic engineering has to face in its present phase of development.

Golden Rice

The creation of a new transgenic variety of rice whose grains contained provitamin A was first reported in the year 2000. Although the content of provitamin A, 1.6 µg/g (micrograms per gram) of grain, was significantly less than the level required for proper nutrition, the crucial first step had been made. Here was proof of a new breeding approach which could then be used for further testing and optimization.

Because the immediate physiological precursor of the pro-vitamin was missing in the source plant variety, the transfer of at least two additional genes was necessary to complement the missing biosynthetic steps. Despite this complexity and the correspondingly extensive research and development effort, the provitamin content was increased to approximately 30 µg/g within only a few years (Fig. 28, color plate VII). Salim Al-Babili and Peter Beyer have written a detailed account of the individual steps in *Golden Rice – five years on the road – five years to go?*

Golden Rice differs from all the products of plant genetic engineering (pp. 135ff.) mentioned thus far in several important points. These specific points, as well as those that generally apply to transgenic plants, must be taken into consideration as development continues:

- the new trait is based on the transfer of not only one, but several genes that are dependent on each other in their interactions;
- the new product is part of the human diet (in contrast, for example, to Bt cotton);
- the materials and procedures used for the gene transfer are protected by numerous extensive patents;
- the target group are poor small farmers and the populations of developing countries supplied by them;
- most of the developing countries in question have very different legal regulations for the application of genetic engineering;
- the new trait has to be crossed into locally adapted varieties for cultivation in developing countries;
- and finally, traditional eating habits have a great influence on the acceptance of unaccustomed types of food.

The transfer of two or more genes was necessary because the last precursor in the rice endosperm (the edible part of the rice grain) could be up to five biosynthetic steps away from provitamin A, depending on the type and origin of the genes. Although the missing genes can be isolated from different sources, every conceivable combination of genes has to be individually tested to determine whether it has a positive or negative effect on the outcome. The increase in the provitamin content mentioned above, from 1.6 to 30 µg/g, is the result of such attempts at optimization, which are by no means exhausted and may even lead to greater increases if deemed necessary.

Because it serves as a direct part of the human diet, the gene-technology assisted development of provitamin A-containing grains of rice which were previously provitamin-free is subject to especially strict testing. It is particularly important to make sure that the provitamin is able to perform its function in the human body without any side effects.

Additional criteria are "bioavailability" and "bioefficiency," i.e. the nutritional effectiveness of the provitamins that are ingested with food. The human body's absorption of provitamin A and its conversion to vitamin A are both strongly dependent on the composition of the diet, especially on the type and quantity of attendant fat as a solubilizer. If the tests currently performed prove that the effectiveness roughly corresponds to that of an average mixed diet (1:12), then the current value of about 30 μg/g would be sufficient.

In view of the high costs of developing a transgenic variety, poor small farmers in developing countries can only be reached with unusual and unconventional means. Most of these people are not even able to pay for the comparatively low-priced seed of traditional rice cultivars. Therefore, a path that excluded corporate profits had to be chosen from the outset.

The solution consisted of a unique form of cooperation between researchers, private foundations, the private sector, and governments. The first step was made by scientists in publicly funded (German and Swiss) universities, where they produced the prototype of a transgenic rice plant in an elaborate and long-term research project. A substantial part of the funding was provided by the Rockefeller Foundation.

Further development into varieties with a steadily increasing provitamin A content was supported by a seed company that was prepared to deliver the improved product free of charge under certain conditions. One condition was the agreement on the part of numerous patent holders to forgo royalties for materials and methods if the product were used by poor farmers.

Patent protection would otherwise have made the free delivery of seeds impossible. It was therefore important to convince all of the parties concerned of the intended humanitarian solution. To this end the "Golden Rice Humanitarian Board" was founded, an honorary committee of internationally experienced representatives from science, industry, humanitarian foundations, foreign aid agencies, and international rice research institutes. Negotiations resulted in a unique solution: All of the participating companies and patent holders agreed to forgo profits as long as the annual income of the recipient small farmers remained below US$10,000.

With this result a high hurdle had indeed been taken, but it was not the last. An additional difficulty proved to be the existence of different laws and implementing regulations in every one of the potentially affected developing countries with regard to the use of transgenic plants.

National legal regulations for genetic engineering and its implementation determine whether – and if so, under what conditions – transgenic plants are to be licensed for commercial use. However, they seldom reflect the needs of the starving and malnourished, but instead the wishes and influence of interest groups, including powerful international trading partners and their governments.

Hardly any less important is the acceptance of genetically modified food by policymakers and the general public. In the end they have a mutual influence on each other, as laws and regulations concerning risk assessment paradoxically appear to the population as an indication of potential danger, rather than creating a feeling of increased security. This does nothing more than reinforce fears that have already arisen from a lack of objective knowledge. As a result, the licensing requirements for Golden Rice are elaborate and time-consuming almost everywhere – despite the pressing health problems.

Crossing the new trait into locally adapted varieties is the last step leading to actual use by those in need. Several national and international rice research institutes provide the best conditions for this effort. They possess suitable breeding material and have the necessary on-site experience. Above all, however, as publicly funded institutes they are non-profit organizations and thus in a position to guarantee that farmers have access to the product free of charge.

And yet, the extent to which the product will be readily accepted continues to depend on the strength of traditional eating habits.

Traditional eating habits determine the acceptance of uncommon food to a great extent, even in times of famine. I will return to this astonishing observation at a later point (p. 229). Experience from other cases cautions us that the readiness to eat yellow instead of white rice cannot be taken for granted everywhere.

These last three steps are presently being pursued with priority: the fulfilment of national licensing criteria that often vary greatly from one country to another, the transfer of new traits to locally used rice varieties, and the overcoming of possible problems with acceptance. It is still too early for conclusive results or a reliable estimate of when the first practical successes will occur.

Even if Golden Rice is able to completely meet the intended goal of eliminating provitamin A deficiency, this will merely represent a solution to one of several problems with the quality of traditional rice varieties. In order to correct the other deficits, the Gates Foundation has now provided considerable resources for an extensive subsequent project to be conducted by the "ProVitaMinRice" Consortium.

The artificial term *ProVitaMinRice* summarizes the project's goals: Developing *rice* varieties that, through improved quality or improved bioavailability of *pro*teins, *vita*mins, and *min*erals, have the greatest possible nutritional value. This includes:

1. increasing the relatively low protein content (in comparison with wheat) using proven genetic engineering methods, and simultaneously enhancing the amounts of essential amino acids (p. 91);
2. increasing the vitamin E content in addition to that of provitamin A, with the expectation that this will improve the physiological stability and the bioavailability of provitamin A;
3. increasing the content of bioavailable iron (against anemia) as well as investigating the mechanisms of bioavailability of iron and zinc (to strengthen, among others, the immune system) as a prerequisite for the development of corresponding breeding strategies;
4. crossing the transgenic prototypes with local rice varieties and obtaining licensing approval for their cultivation.

A project this extensive and demanding can only be accomplished through the collaboration of partners who are especially competent in their particular fields. The consortium is accordingly composed of several German, American, and Chinese research teams as well as rice research and rice breeding institutes from India, Vietnam, and the Philippines.

The future will prove whether and to what extent these individual goals are attainable. However, after the experience with Golden Rice, these goals appear neither unrealistic nor even utopian. The highly nutritional wheat kernel serves as a paragon.

With this example in mind, it is not difficult to imagine other cases of quality improvement in our food sources. The initial focus will be on similar developments with other major crop plants. Concrete projects with cassava, sorghum, and some banana species, all of which show signs of deficiency with unbalanced diets, are already underway. Another important breeding goal is the qualitatively improved composition of plant oil in oleiferous plants.

The more successful and convincing the contributions of genetic engineering are with regard to these efforts, the sooner other projects will follow that would be equally difficult or impossible to pursue with conventional breeding alone.

Yield Potential

The amount of yield a crop plant produces depends on two complementary conditions: the potential for yield as predisposed in the plant's genetic constitution, and the external conditions under which this potential comes to fruition, i.e. the climate, soil conditions, fertilization, plant protection, and the supply of water. Many of these issues have been addressed above.

One of the rare giant leaps in an increase in yield potential through a single trait modification was the successful breeding of dwarf wheat and rice in the 1960s. This mutation caused the redirection of a large share of metabolic activity from stalk to kernel production and thus played a significant role in the precipitous yield increases during the Green Revolution (p. 206).

Two frequently stated breeding goals that could lead to equally high gains are an increase in photosynthetic efficiency and the biological fixation of nitrogen, the latter especially with cereals and some other main food sources. In both cases concrete starting points for breeding programs are not yet in sight; but in view of their potential importance, they should not go unmentioned.

Photosynthesis (the conversion of carbon dioxide and water to energy-rich organic compounds with the help of light energy) comprises a chain of biochemical reactions that occur in all green parts of a plant in special cellular compartments called chloroplasts. Chlorophyll, the light-absorbing pigment, is the most salient component of chloroplasts, which gives leaves and stems their characteristic green color.

Photosynthesis is exceedingly important in terms of the plant's yield potential. In comparison to many other biochemical reactions, however, it has a low level of efficiency that has been little improved to date, despite great efforts by breeders. Theoretically it is hard to conceive of a more effective increase in yield potential than through increasing the efficiency of photosynthesis.

Numerous groups of researchers are therefore extremely eager to find out why this efficiency is not greater and whether a clue about possible genetic modifications can be inferred from their findings. Opinions about the prospects of success vary greatly. Skeptics point to the fact that photosynthesis was a product of biological evolution several billion years ago. Naturally occurring mutations would long since have led to increased efficiency if a possibility existed.

Comprehensive knowledge of the genetic basis and the molecular mechanisms of action of photosynthesis is required to remove this uncertainty in evaluating possible starting points for breeding efforts.

Legumes (Fabaceae) are among the few types of plants that are able to directly fix atmospheric nitrogen. In association with nitrogen fixing bacteria, they form a highly specialized symbiotic organ. This organ, or *nodule*, offers the bacteria a protected space where they can live, reproduce, "work," and supply the plant with valuable nitrogenous compounds. As compensation the plant provides the bacteria with products of photosynthesis, i.e. with organically bound carbon.

Two important conditions must be met for the formation of nodules: the nitrogen-fixing bacteria have to be recognized as such by the plant, and the plant's normal defensive reactions against microorganisms must be suppressed. This requires a highly specialized and coordinated form of communication between the two organisms through species-specific signal molecules and surface structures.

Plants that are not specialized in this regard, such as all types of cereals and most other food plants, are as a rule unable to form such symbioses. But just this sort of increase in yield potential would be of enormous ecological and economic benefit in view of the large input of synthetic nitrogen fertilizers.

It is extremely unlikely that conventional breeding alone could ever achieve such a goal. In addition to increasing the efficiency of photosynthesis, nitrogen fixation is therefore often referred to as one of the great future dreams of plant genetic engineering. Here again, detailed knowledge of the molecular mechanisms and their genetic foundation is indispensable.

Vitality and Yield Reliability

The overriding importance of plant vitality and a reliable yield in agriculture have already been discussed in Chapter 3. Although the two terms describe different phenomena, they are nonetheless closely related. Vitality is the general fitness and adaptability to the environment as well as species- and variety-specific performance and endurance strength; yield reliability is the practical result of these features under agricultural conditions.

From this complex description of vitality it follows that a large number of characteristics are at stake which must be considered in breeding. And here as well, the complexity can only be indicated by looking at a few typical examples. In doing so I will once again give precedence to such cases where plant genetic engineering plays a major role or is very likely to do so.

The first two cases describe new genetic engineering approaches to the breeding of fungal and viral resistance. Two additional examples concern goals whose practical implementation is still pending, but which are nonetheless of great significance: drought and salt tolerance.

Fungal resistance is an important criterion for vitality and reliable yields, particularly in temperate climatic zones like those found in Europe. A good example is the potato. Its most important pathogen (Phytophthora infestans, an oomycete resembling a fungus), which causes potato blight, first appeared in Europe during the 1840s and in several successive years destroyed a majority of Europe's potato crop. Millions of people starved at this time or were forced to emigrate.

Even today resistance breeding for potato blight is strongly impaired because new virulent strains of the pathogen are continuously formed through mutations. For breeding purposes either monogenically inherited forms of resistance (which are only effective for a short time) or longer lasting polygenically inherited forms (which are difficult to use in breeding) are available, if at all, either from wild types or from other cultivars. The problem is considerably aggravated by modern mass-cultivation methods of potato farming (p. 80).

Because of these difficulties a prototype of a transgenic potato variety with a new form of disease resistance was developed using genetic engineering methods. Resistance is based on an artificial mechanism that never occurred in evolution and for which there are numerous possible modifications due to the current state of promoter and structural gene research.

The result was a potato plant on which the reproduction of Phytophthora infestans was greatly reduced in comparison with the source plant (Fig. 29, color plate VII). This effect might well have led to a reduction in the spread of the disease under field conditions.

The project pursued three goals: (1) the development of new mechanisms of resistance that would be difficult to overcome through pathogen mutation; (2) the designing of mechanisms that would be effective against a wide variety of fungi and bacteria, similar to broadly effective antibiotics; and (3) the development of a transgenic prototype for the actual breeding of resistant potato varieties.

The project was financed with public funds from the former German Federal Ministry for Research and Technology in the hope of being able to at least partially dispense with the use of environmentally damaging pesticides should the project prove to be a success. Despite this environmental policy objective, however, the first officially approved field trial was destroyed by genetic engineering opponents before the scientific evaluation had even begun (Fig. 30, color plate VII). As a result the project was discontinued.

For virus resistance there are often no known naturally occurring resistance genes and conventional breeding attempts have been mostly unsuccessful to date. Hence, breeders were also inclined to investigate the production of transgenic plants, which in this case contained a gene for the expression of a viral protein. In doing so, breeders took advantage of the phenomenon that the replication of viruses is prevented by their own coat proteins as long as these are freely available in the plant cells.

Because viruses are not independent cellular organisms, they are dependent on reproduction within suitable host organisms. In comparison to the cells of their hosts, viruses are very simply constructed and consist merely of the genetic information for their own structural components, including a protective protein coat, and a few additional functions.

As the virus replicates in the regular manner, the coat protein is produced in precisely the amount needed for the assembly of the individual parts. If the coat protein is already present in the plant and thus occurring in excess amounts, however, it prevents replication of the virus.

Almost complete virus resistance has been achieved in some plants through the transfer of a gene encoding a viral coat protein by genetic engineering. According to investigations carried out thus far, this type of resistance is even partially directed toward other kinds of viruses that possess different coat proteins. Some of the more closely analyzed transgenic plants exhibited neither growth nor yield reductions when compared with the corresponding control plants, even when they contained relatively large amounts of viral protein in comparison to their own cellular proteins.

The first practical example is a virus-resistant papaya variety that has increasingly taken over the market in Hawaii since it was first used commercially in 1998. Transgenic papaya varieties are practically the only varieties used on the island now. They contain a gene for the coat protein of the papaya ringspot potyvirus (PRSV), which rapidly spread among the most important growing areas on Hawaii in the early 1990s, destroying a large part of the harvest.

By coincidence, and after several years of research, the first field tests of the transgenic prototype were being run when the first substantial virus infections occurred. Within a few years cultivatable transgenic varieties (Fig. 31, color plate VIII) which fulfilled all licensing criteria proved to be so successful that they were quickly able to compensate for the temporary loss of the papaya harvest. These varieties were not only PRSV resistant, but they even provided higher yields than the original varieties. Further details are provided by Dennis Gonsalves in *Transgenic Papaya in Hawaii and Beyond*.

Drought tolerance (or to be more precise, drought stress tolerance) is an essential prerequisite for agricultural productivity, particularly in regions with low average precipitation or long and persistent periods of dryness. The rapidly expanding Sahel Belt and growing arid regions around the Aral Sea, which itself is drying up, are striking examples of how this problem is becoming increasingly dramatic. As I will be discussing these and other specific cases below (p. 222), I will limit myself here to a few remarks about the state of breeding.

Conventional breeding will continue to contribute significantly to the problem of drought tolerance. Innovative genetic engineering approaches first require that more precise knowledge is gained from basic research. The demanding complexity of this research area is due to the special role of water in the plant's physiology.

On the one hand, water is the universal solvent for all metabolic activities performed by plants, including the absorption of all nutrients through the root system and the long-distance transport of metabolites from the roots to the leaf tips and vice versa. On the other hand water itself is an important nutrient needed in great quantities as a substrate for photosynthesis. And finally, plants regulate their temperature balance almost exclusively through the evaporation of water, which thus indirectly regulates their metabolism and growth.

To maintain a correct equilibrium requires a fine-tuned hydrologic balance among all parts of the system both within the plant and between the plant and its surroundings. Most plants are overexerted when this meticulous mechanism is faced with a constantly high level of drought stress.

Evolution has responded with the creation of several plant species, such as sedum, cacti, and camel thorn, that are specifically adapted to different types of dry locations. These plants have developed essentially three different mechanisms for dealing with drought stress: The reduction of water loss through modification of the surface structures, increased water absorption through a widely branching root system, or the ability to adjust the metabolism such that it functions properly even when the water content is greatly reduced.

Investigating these mechanisms is scientifically appealing because of the complexity of their interactions, but offers no easy answers. The extent to which the results of this research will open up new possibilities for breeding with genetic engineering is not yet clear. Any progress, however, is potentially of multiple value due to the additional close links between drought tolerance, salt tolerance, and to a certain degree frost tolerance. In each case the loss of water from cells has to be countered with a proper remedy.

Salt tolerance is not only related to drought tolerance in terms of the plant's hydrologic balance, but is also becoming more and more important to breeders. The connection to a balanced supply of water is evident: Almost all nutrients from the soil are mineral salts dissolved in water. They cannot rise above or fall below a certain concentration inside or outside the plant without adversely affecting its metabolism.

Freshwater is used to irrigate plants; and although it has

a much lower level of salinity than salt water, it still contains appreciable amounts of mineral salts. A high percentage of the water diverted to fields evaporates, especially in warm climatic zones, and salt accumulates on the soil's surface, sometimes even forming a firm crust.

Another form of salt stress that does not directly affect the hydrologic balance is caused by the release of toxic aluminum salts due to soil acidification, or by the input of heavy metal salts from industrial processes. In these cases stress is caused by the immediate toxicity and not because of dehydration. This is also an increasing problem in agriculture.

Only a few plants that possess specific tolerance mechanisms can manage in such situations. Their increased tolerance may be based on different principles, e.g. on reduced absorption, special excretory mechanisms, or increased storage capacity. In all of these cases too little is known about the underlying mechanisms in order to be able to derive promising breeding strategies.

A reliable yield does not end with the harvesting of a field. Large quantities of stored harvest are lost to insect pests or pathogen infections, especially in the hot and humid climates of tropical regions. These losses are particularly great in areas that already suffer from food shortages. In order to effectively solve this problem resistance breeding has to go beyond the approaches already discussed and has to intensify breeding efforts for post-harvest pest control and pathogen resistance – not to mention improved storage and transport conditions (see Chapter 8).

Vaccines in Foodstuffs

Plants whose edible parts contain either vaccines against infectious diseases that are difficult to check or other medically effective substances constitute a fundamentally new goal for breeders. The greatest progress has been made in the development of transgenic plants containing vaccines for those kinds of diseases that are particularly common in developing countries.

Vaccines that stimulate the body's own immune system to produce antibodies have traditionally consisted of either dead or weakened pathogens or of antigens isolated from them. All of these vaccines have to be injected or taken orally, which is a complicated and often nearly impossible procedure in many developing countries, especially in the case of large-scale immunization programs.

A substantially better solution would be vaccines contained in food that affected population groups already consume on a daily basis. To achieve this, viral or bacterial genes from a pathogenic organism were transferred to plants which then produced those proteins or protein fragments that functioned as antigens. Based on the successful immunization of laboratory animals, several of these projects are now at a stage where clinical tests are being run.

In the early phases of this new development breeders first concentrated on plants and pathogens which were easily accessible in methodological terms, e.g. transgenic potatoes that have an immunizing effect on intestinal infections or hepatitis B. Owing to the results thus far, the likelihood that this spectrum will rapidly grow is great. Antigen-containing bananas and rice grains, the latter of which are also useful for the immunotherapy treatment of pollen allergies, are among the projects that are especially advanced.

Developing Countries as the Main Target Group

Developing countries have been emphasized as the primary target group in this chapter several times. They will also play a significant role in several of the following chapters. Improvements in food quality (e.g. Golden Rice), drought and salt tolerance, pest and pathogen resistance, and food vaccines are projects which should especially benefit the populations of developing countries (a detailed overview of current research projects with transgenic plants in developing countries is provided by Joel I. Cohen in an article published in 2005 entitled *Poorer nations turn to publicly developed GM crops*).

Two very different reasons prompt me to implicitly stress this once again: firstly, a lack of awareness (outside those areas directly affected) of the dramatic situation of steadily growing numbers of people who suffer from malnutrition and starvation while the overall population continues to grow; and secondly, the increasing importance of plant genetic engineering efforts to find countermeasures. The emphasis placed on both issues – the problem of hunger and the potential of genetic engineering – in the status report and subsidy programs of internationally operating institutions such as the World Bank, various subsidiary organizations, governmental foreign aid organizations and private foundations, is impressive.

The remarkable appeal by the director of the "ISAAA AfriCenter" in Nairobi, Florence Wambugu, in *Why Africa needs agricultural biotech* begins with the sentence, "There is urgent need for the development and use of agricultural biotechnology in Africa to help to counter famine, environmental degradation and poverty," and ends with the statement: "In the past, many foreign donors funded high-input projects, which have failed to be sustainable because they have failed to address social and economic issues such as changes in cultural practice. The criticism of agri-biotech products in Europe is based on socioeconomic issues and not food safety issues, and no evidence so far justifies the opinion of some in Europe that Africa should be excluded from transgenic crops. Africans can speak for themselves."

Summary

Two main goals have determined the breeding of food plants since the very beginning of agriculture: the quality and the quantity of the human diet. A third important goal, environmental protection, has recently been added, particularly the breeding of plants which demand fewer pesticides. On the one hand, the amount of crop yield is dependent on genetically determined factors (yield potential and vitality) and, on the other, on the conditions of cultivation.

While the maintenance of cultivars is a universal field of activity for breeders, the majority of cultivar-specific traits differ in importance, depending on regional requirements and conditions. Plant genetic engineering has opened up new possibilities for many specific breeding goals that cannot be achieved with traditional methods. Several examples were explained in more detail: nutritionally improved rice, new forms of fungal and virus resistance, drought and salt tolerance, as well as food vaccines. The main target group is the developing countries.

Major progress in breeding is based on the results of basic research in molecular biology. This research continues to have great potential for innovation.

7 Ethical Evaluation of Genetic Engineering

Debates about the responsible use of genetic engineering are more common outside the discipline than discussions about its substance and its goals. There is a profound reason for this discrepancy: a general and deep-seated fear of an irresponsible way of dealing with new technological possibilities. This fear is not surprising at a time when science and technology are making revolutionary progress while the ethics involved with this revolution have hardly been addressed.

This kind of disparity reveals just how much we follow old and instinctive survival strategies despite all of the alleged rationality of our actions. The motto "who dares wins" (or in science and technology, "Wisdom is born of experience" and "He knows the water well who has waded through it") was certainly an essential reason why the species *Homo sapiens* has been so successful in surviving and asserting itself. And now, after such a long – subjectively perceived – period of "eternal" validity of this type of strategy, it proves to be very difficult to apparently reverse it. The successful principle of audacity has abruptly been turned into an audacity-inhibiting principle of responsibility. Is this a complete about-face?

Yes and no. Yes, because science and technology have reached a level where each venture that proves to be too big has repercussions that go far beyond the perpetrators. This did not begin with genetic engineering, but it generally requires a greater sense of responsibility with each further step. No, because it is not about a change from one principle to another, opposing one, but merely about a smoother accentuation of parts that belong together. Science, technology, and responsibility are closely linked. Genetic engineering is the youngest of a long series of technological innovations that reinforce this necessity.

The philosopher Hans Jonas has taken an especially thorough stand on the relationship between science, technology and responsibility in his book *Technik, Medizin und Ethik* (*On Technology, Medicine, and Ethics*, not yet translated into English). His formulation of the "Principle of Responsibility" primarily refers to genetic engineering. Particularly worthy of note in this context is his discussion of utopia, which in its socio-political manifestation assumes an idealized image of humanity and therefore sets no secure limits for the development of science and technology. In this respect, the "Principle of Responsibility" is not only an analysis of the direct interdependency of technology and responsibility, but also an answer to Ernst Bloch's *Principle of Hope*, with its Marxist-utopian component.

And with this an important point of view has come to the fore. An ethical question that is as oriented toward practical consequences as that of the responsible application of genetic engineering in plant breeding has to be based on existing realities and beware of utopian ideals.

An ethical evaluation begins with the source of the new technology, science, and ends where each individual participates directly or indirectly in the decision making about our common future.

Science and Responsibility

Science is the search for and enhancement of knowledge. One of its attributes is progress: Science asks pertinent questions in accordance with the state of knowledge and with its answers increases knowledge, which thus inevitably progresses. By taking responsibility for itself, science also unavoidably takes responsibility for progress. All new scientific knowledge – and even more so its practical application – once again raises the question of how (and not if) science assumes its responsibility. Only when combined will scientific knowledge and its responsible handling constitute true progress.

Martin Buber described the elusive concept of "responsibility" in his essay *Zwiesprache: Traktat vom dialogischen Leben* (Dialogue: Treatise about a Dialogical Life) in an especially beautiful and comprehensive manner. Everyone is responsible for everything with which he or she has a conscious or unconscious relationship. One is responsible in that one gives concrete answers: "Genuine responsibility only exists where there are true answers … for those things that happen to one, for what one sees, hears, and feels." "A dog looked at you, you are responsible for its look; a child seized your hand, you are responsible for its touch; a crowd of people stirs around you, you are responsible for their distress."

We should continue in the context of this book: Nearly one billion people are starving, we are responsible for their privation. Millions die each year as a consequence of famine, we are responsible for their indigence. Our environment is being smothered by our continued population growth, we are responsible for our disregard of nature. The Earth has been wounded through our plundering of its resources, we are responsible for our lifestyle. We are aware of the urgent need for effective action, we are responsible for our inaction.

But what is responsibility specifically in the context of science – who is responsible, and for what?

For the following discussion we need a definition that is as comprehensive as possible. "Who" is every scientist as an individual as well as science as an acting whole; "what" is the mode and the subject of scientific activity, as well as the way the results are dealt with. All scientists are – to the same degree as all other people – personally responsible for their own professional, and in this case scientific, activities, for the quality of their work, and for informing the public about the possible repercussions this may have on them.

While taking individual freedom into account, quality is ensured within each field by way of technical evaluation by scientists themselves, who thereby assume joint responsibility towards the general public. In doing so every scientist is free to choose his or her field of research within commonly set and generally accepted boundaries. These boundaries may be of a purely practical nature, for instance a common topic-related goal of a research team, or a financial priority set according to superordinate aspects. Often, however, they are also legally or ethically imposed, for example a ban on unnecessary use of experimental animals or genetic engineering experiments on the human germline.

The molecular biological prerequisites for the development of genetic engineering were the results of pure, purpose-free basic research. None of these results was predictable, and certainly not genetic engineering as the sum total of its various components. They were not looked for and consequently found (invented), but were rather discovered in a pure search for knowledge and later combined and further developed into a technology.

Every scientist is responsible for his search for knowledge about nature and ourselves – or to be more precise, for the subject, the quality, and the methods of this search. (Pure search for knowledge fundamentally excludes a practical purpose. Financial profit is a purpose and therefore application-oriented, thus limiting the possibilities of enhancing knowledge.)

As a rule basic research at universities and comparable research institutes are financed with public funds. It is therefore conducted under the condition that the results be made available to the public, i.e. published in a freely accessible professional journal. Basic research may indeed be unrestricted – within the boundaries mentioned above – but internal quality control and the allocation of funding requires the regular publication of previous results. In this respect, responsibility for the type and subject of research within a particular area of expertise is guaranteed.

Scientists are, however, responsible for more than just the type and subject of their specific activity. They are also – as competent experts – jointly responsible for the utilization of their knowledge. They practice this primarily by informing the public about the opportunities and risks of developments in their field, whether it involves problem areas such as agriculture and environmental protection, radiation therapy and radiation risks, or the synthesis of pharmaceuticals and toxic chemical waste. What matters is to evaluate both on a comparative basis: to do something or not do it, the application or non-application of a method for a particular purpose.

In practice, however, science can barely fulfill this kind of responsibility to the general public. In democratic societies at least, the public is formally (due to "public" tax revenues) the sponsor of basic research. Because of this relationship it has a right to be informed, but it is quite inept at executing it. This problem is of such great importance, particularly in the case of an innovative field such as genetic engineering, that it will be dealt with in a separate section (p. 191). However, it is necessary to precede this discourse with a somewhat more detailed analysis of the present situation.

Technology, Economics, the State, and Politics

For the majority of those who as the "general public" are not directly involved, there are several anonymous links in the chain of executing powers that stand between basic science and themselves: the application (technology), utilization (the economy), administration (the government), and control (politics). Most people are thus not aware of just how much this perceived anonymity represents unawareness of their own role.

The cultural philosopher José Ortega y Gasset wrote his famous essay *The Revolt of the Masses* while under the influence of impending fascism in Europe. In it he analyses modern mass-man and reaches the conclusion that, "there will not be found amongst all the representatives of the actual period a single group whose attitude to life is not limited to believing that it has all the rights and none of the obligations ... after one or two twists, its state of mind will consist, decisively, in ignoring all obligations, and in feeling itself ... possessed of unlimited rights."

It is a fatal abandonment (and one's own fault) of each person's individual freedom if one demands responsibility from all other links of the chain without demanding anything of oneself. As long as people look for responsibility only in "science," "technology," "the economy," "the government," or "politics" (where of course it *also* lies) they relinquish power as they give up responsibility.

The power of the individual consists of jointly deciding – by voting for politicians – about the government and the economy and therefore about the application or non-application of a particular technology. Among a crowd of people, the individual does not count for much, but together individuals make decisions about everything. The less informed they are, the weaker they are, and hence unsure and more easily influenced.

This argument should underline the connection between the power and the responsibility of the individual, but should not distract from the concentration of both with select groups of people in science, technology, the economy, government, and politics. The temporarily accentuated role of intermediary and advocate, above all for politicians, is particularly voiced through a limited legislative period.

A parliamentary initiative to have the risks and opportunities of genetic engineering evaluated by the Commission of Inquiry of the Tenth German Bundestag (the Lower House of the German Parliament) corresponded to this role.

Risks and Opportunities of Genetic Engineering

In 1987, after several years of analysis by experts, this commission published a final report which was more than 400 pages long. The title, *Chancen und Risiken der Gentechnologie* (Risks and Opportunities of Genetic Engineering) has certainly led to the fact that these two terms are often used together. The contrasting of two concepts which are so open-ended – risks and opportunities – reveals just how much both the expected positive as well as the feared negative aspects largely represented perceptions of the future at the time.

Genetic engineering was developed because of its opportunities. Meanwhile it has proved to be an unequivocal benefit in biological and medical research (cancer, AIDS, and hereditary diseases), in the production of pharmaceuticals, and in the breed-ing of crops (p. 130ff.). Therefore, it is now quite easy to list the possible advantages of using genetic engineering. Estimating the risks, on the other hand, is considerably more speculative. Thus this should be done in the form of a catalog of questions and answers derived from many discussions. First of all, however, it would be useful to briefly analyze the concept of risk and the general state of knowledge.

Similar to the pair of concepts of opportunity and benefit, risk and harm stand for the boundary between possibility and certainty. In this sense, risk is a venture that includes the possibil-ity of harm. It may be helpful, however, to realize that a benefit can always represent harm in another respect: intensive agricul-ture benefits those people now alive, it harms natural biodiversity and future generations; fungal or insect resistance benefits plants and humans, but harms the affected organisms. As a basic prin-ciple, therefore, opportunities and risks cannot be completely separated from one another.

This lack of clarity runs through all areas of ethics and partic-ularly impedes discussions about the value of risk and the admis-sible degree of willingness to take risks. The senseless concept of "calculated risk" is especially detrimental. By definition a risk is not calculable. No one, however, would question the fact that life without risk is inconceivable.

For the continuing discussion I assume that a discernable risk of genetic engineering will be avoided through proper consider-ation of all its advantages and disadvantages. The fact that it will unavoidably result in a discretionary decision is a problem risk analysis shares with all other aspects of practical ethics. Efforts to find out as much about the situation as possible and to make an unbiased judgment therefore become even more important.

Fear and Ignorance

Making an unbiased judgement presupposes the *ability* to judge: relevant basic knowledge and independent thinking. Both are mutually dependent on one another. Basic knowledge is not specialized knowledge, but a part of general education. It differs from specialized knowledge in one essential point: it does not go into detail but instead deals with the fundamentals of our living conditions and their connections. Where this basic knowledge is absent, opinions and fears rule the day instead of balanced judgments.

A concrete example from plant genetic engineering can serve as an illustration. Anyone who wishes to make a judgment about genetic modifications in plants has to know that plants – like all other organisms – contain thousands of different genes. The total number can be slightly increased or decreased with the help of genetic engineering. What this means, however, is that a "gene tomato" has not suddenly been created from an allegedly gene-free tomato. Furthermore, a proper judgment about plant genetic engineering requires a basic knowledge of the fact that in principle a similar process occurs with conventional breeding, and that with or without genetic engineering a significant part of our food consists of genes (which are nutritionally valuable!).

When this simple piece of basic knowledge finally determines the majority of judgments about plant genetic engineering, such nonsensical terms such as "gene-free zone" and "gene food" will lose their ability to cause fear out of ignorance.

'Fear is a poor counselor' is a common saying. This statement may or may not be true, but in any case it is incomplete. Fear is a valuable, and in certain situations, life-saving evolutionary achievement. It is the instinctive reaction to insecurity when confronted with an unknown. Thus fear does not necessarily have to be a poor counselor. But it nonetheless remains incomplete if the implicit counsel is not heeded: remedy the lack of knowledge and allay the insecurity that causes the fear.

Germany is a typical example of an export-dependent industrial country which frequently emphasizes its lack of material resources and its wealth of intellectual capacity, especially in the natural sciences and technology. It is therefore alarming when basic knowledge about the natural sciences is so inadequate that in discussions about genetic engineering the question is often raised about what will happen when "I eat a gene."

In the final chapter I will address the fact that the future of plant genetic engineering will not be determined by scientists, but by society as a whole. Sound independent judgments are needed and not easily manipulated opinions determined by fear and a lack of knowledge. The need for a content-related (and not only bureaucratic and administrative) educational reform is therefore all the more urgent in order to successfully raise the general ability of people to make their own judgments.

The European Perspective

Public opinion of plant genetic engineering is largely negative, particularly in Europe's industrial countries. The majority of critical statements reveal that fear due to ignorance cannot be the only reason. In addition to communication difficulties between science and the general public, which I will refer to in more detail (p. 191), a blinkered point of view is obviously a fundamental factor.

From a European perspective there is no lack of food, but on the contrary rather a lack of political decision making to end costly overproduction. The barely manageable diversity of luxury goods and temptations in supermarkets, including never-ending shelves of select food for dogs, cats, hamsters, and birds, merely reinforces this view.

In Europe exceptional conditions prevail with regard to agricultural productivity compared to many other regions where a large part of the population is starving. This is often not recognized, even though Europeans travel the world as tourists. The vacation "paradises" are too far away, physically as well as mentally, from the drought-stricken or flooded famine areas for visitors to notice.

The willingness of relief organizations such as *World Hunger Aid*, *Bread for the World*, *Misereor*, and many others to donate is immense, and is helpful and commendable. And yet, how can average Europeans or North Americans living in a constitutional and welfare state understand the dire situation of a poverty-stricken small farming family with few rights in Ethiopia, Zambia, Haiti, Myanmar or Bangladesh during a series of famines, floods or droughts? And how should they understand that an abundance of children means having workers, old-age security, and perhaps even hope for a more tolerable future?

In the next chapter I will discuss this in more concrete terms, especially the fact that an effective long-term solution has to involve helping such people to help themselves. Europe, North America, and Japan are especially called upon in this regard.

The European perspective presumably contains yet another moral and psychological element. Many 21st century Europeans have become aware of the consequences of the conquest and economic exploitation of entire parts of the world since the end of the 15th century. Obvious signs of this new awareness were numerous critical media reports and the noticeably reserved statements by politicians on the occasion of the 500th anniversary of the "discovery of America".

This is the direction a nearly stereotypical question presumably also takes: Isn't plant genetic engineering just going to benefit industrialized countries, once again at the expense of developing countries? Experiences to the contrary (p. 137) and ongoing projects (pp. 149ff.) which disprove these misgivings are apparently too new to play a role in the general consciousness.

It is especially difficult to answer the question of why the view of plant genetic engineering is so critical in most parts of Europe, even though the technology was partially developed here and the standard of basic research in this field continues to be recognized around the world.

Perhaps Kurt Tucholsky, a deeply concerned German author and citizen, pointed us in a direction that contains more truth and thoughtfulness about his people than it reveals on the surface when he wrote, "Even when a German has nothing, he still has his doubts and concerns." I am not competent enough to illuminate this sentence in psychological terms, although the ambiguity of the word "concern" is obvious. With this in mind, it seems plausible that the fatal historical misstep from an exceptionally optimistic and successful phase of constructive concern with progress in science and technology at the beginning of the 20th century led to an equally unusual phase of completely unconcerned, unscrupulous and destructive dictatorship and now to a phase of deep concern and restraint.

It is possible that Tucholsky was trying to express something much more fundamental: When nothing more than doubts and concerns remain, assuredness, self-confidence, and the ability and willingness to make a clear judgment will be lacking.

Feared Consequences

The following selection of frequently asked questions about plant genetic engineering is a clear expression of the general concern regarding this widely unknown type of scientific and technological development.

By keeping my answers and comments to each question brief, I will attempt to limit them to their essential core. In order to address every relevant aspect, however, I will have to answer twice in some cases. Here in this section I will address each question directly and as far as possible from a scientific point of view. And below I will indirectly incorporate some additional answers (in the form of practical conclusions) to the more application-related questions into the last two chapters of the book.

What will happen if humans interfere with the natural evolution of the species through artificial gene transfer?

This question (one of the most common) is very complex. It can be divided into three parts. Two parts are of a general nature, while the third addresses biological science. The first part is: Should humans be allowed to deliberately interfere with natural evolution? The answer can only be a pragmatic one: Apparently so, as we have been doing this very effectively (and with increasing intensity) since the beginning of the Neolithic Revolution through the breeding of plants, animals, and microorganisms.

Apart from this historical fact, we ourselves are a part and a product of this evolution. The massive growth of our own population has either greatly influenced the evolution of nearly all other species directly or indirectly, or has even led to their extinction. The question should therefore be how much – and not whether – we should be allowed to interfere with, evolution or even want to. My personal answer to this question can be found in Chapter 9.

The second part of the question adds a new dimension to the first: Should humans be allowed to use *genetic engineering* to interfere with the evolution of the species? The answer to this part of the question cannot be pragmatically derived from our past cultural history. This is the real core question, and as such will play an important role in this and the following chapters. Although it cannot be answered by the discipline of science alone, much will depend on the nature of science's answer to the following questions.

The third part of the question is specifically directed toward scientific judgement: Are there scientific reasons which would oppose the artificial transfer of genes as interference with the natural evolution of the species? The answer, a conditional no, will likewise emerge from everything to come.

Is it possible that genes transferred through genetic engineering are able to spread uncontrollably?

As far as we know from the limited experience we have gained thus far, this possibility exists to the same degree as it does for genes that are transferred without human intervention, i.e. within sexual crossing and hybridization barriers. It is therefore important when using transgenic plants outside of laboratories, at least in the beginning, to limit ourselves to such organisms that will not disseminate in the wild in an unwanted and uncontrolled fashion and potentially mix with other cultivars or wild types through sexual crossing.

Incidentally, here it should be noted that humans have spread huge numbers of genes around the world for thousands of years. They have – intentionally or not – spread all ornamental and agricultural plants, animals and other types of organisms, including pests and pathogens, as far and as wide as the climate and other conditions allowed. Every one of these organisms contains thousands of genes in each cell that could potentially be transferred to other individuals or species.

Can genetic engineering be used to create organisms which, intentionally or by chance, have so much vitality that they endanger the existing biodiversity?

This is very hard to imagine, and inconceivable for our highly bred food plants. There have always been particularly vital adaptation strategists, for instance in our day the fly, the rat, and humans themselves. And yet, as far as we know, the biosphere as a whole was never in danger – except presently as a result of our own global threats to the environment.

Increased fitness due to adaptation to continuously changing ecological conditions is, as a rule, only a temporary advantage in a healthy biosphere. Every mutation and every new combination of genes, whether genetically engineered, sexually or otherwise generated, is only one of countless developmental steps, of which only a few – temporarily effective ones – represent the actual progress in natural evolution. The greater the biodiversity, the slighter the chance of endangering it with either genetically engineered or naturally occurring genetic modification.

Is it possible to create biological weapons with genetic engineering?

This is presumably possible; for example, by trying to expand the host spectrum of an animal-specific pathogen such that it attacks humans. However, the mechanisms of infection created during evolution thus far are, even with relatively "simple" pathogens like viruses, so unbelievably sophisticated (AIDS, for example) and the natural possibilities of mutations are so numerous and effective, that using them would very probably lead to more success than an attempt using genetic engineering.

For this reason I feel it is absolutely urgent for biologists to continuously point out the possibility, danger, and vileness of using biological weapons so that worldwide condemnation, with or without genetic engineering, is achieved.

In this context, it is often argued that the mere development of genetic engineering would make it available for such purposes, and even if it were unintentional, it would still be guilty of this possibility. And this guilt would not be lessened by the fact that the same argument could be used for every other type of weapon. If, however, the search for knowledge is part of our cultural development, then guilt is not in the search itself, but in the *application* of that knowledge with *malicious intent*, and in a lack of willingness to accept a degree of responsibility appropriate to the stage of science and technology. Therein lies a certain analogy to the next question.

Does the development of genetic engineering in microorganisms, animals, and plants pave the way for the genetic engineering of humans?

Apart from slight species-specific peculiarities, genetic engineering methods are very much the same for all organisms. The methodological development of this technology will therefore principally lead to possible applications in all areas. This understandably reinforces the widespread fear people have of genetic engineering. This fear has two components: a technical one and an ethical one.

The technical component concerns the possible goals and results of a genetically engineered modification of humans. Because the ethical component is by far the strongest, however, and presently determines our behavior regardless of the technical possibilities, I will limit myself to talking about the ethical part of the question.

Every genetically engineered intervention is a specific genetic modification and thus breeding. The purposeful breeding of humans has presumably never occurred due to ethical reasons – except for a brief attempt by the totalitarian Nazi regime, which tried to purify the Aryan race by negatively breeding out an "inferior genotype." Obviously it was not clear to proponents of this racial fanaticism that they would biologically weaken and endanger their own race through this form of inbreeding (reduction of genetic variability).

Human breeding, i.e. a specific genetic modification or a specific selection of humans, fundamentally violates human dignity because of the valuation associated with it ("improvement," or determination for a specific function).

The ethical reasons for not carrying out human breeding are deeply rooted. They testify to one's own sense of worth as well as to the esteem for others. Seen from an ecological point of view, this placing of value on human individuality corresponds to the general value of preserving genetic variability within populations (p. 62). Breeding humans with the goal of some form of genetic standardization would represent deterioration from both an ethical and a biological point of view – as opposed to the racist definition of "worthless" life.

The responsibility would be unbearable if people were to have a direct influence on their own genetic constitution in order to achieve certain breeding goals. Whether one day the treatment of hereditary diseases through germline modification can and should be exempted is not at issue here. For the time being the human germline must be completely protected by law from any genetic engineering intervention.

On the basis of this position I would like to return to the actual question of whether science can take responsibility for developing a technology for breeding organisms (which have long been bred by other means) that can also be applied to humans, thus indirectly facilitating the possibility of human breeding. The answer can only be a reference to what has been stated earlier in the book: Science is equally responsible for what it does and for what it refrains from doing. Whoever is convinced that for ethical reasons plant breeding with genetic engineering is a goal worth pursuing – for environmental protection as well as for human nutritional needs – cannot refuse his responsibility by referring to the ambivalence of all action.

Doesn't genetic engineering ultimately benefit only multinational industrial corporations – at the expense of the environment and developing countries?

This is also a common question, but it is improperly formulated. It implies that our economic constellations consists of dominating industrial *corporations* on one the one hand, and those that are dependent on them on the other. But this is only the ostensible result of a dividing line which, in reality, lies somewhere else. The actual division lies between economically and politically dominant industrial *countries* and those who are dependent on them.

Multinational industrial corporations are the product, and not the cause, of an economic system that is confirmed (and therefore desired) by a great majority of the population in all politically free industrial countries in a regular cycle of parliamentary elections. The differences among most political parties are unimportant in this regard: Industrial production is one of the mainstays of our prosperity – our tax revenues and our jobs.

Those who do not wish to cede the application of genetic engineering or the subsequent financial profit to industrial corporations have to either rely (mostly in vain) on private, non-profit initiatives (as with Golden Rice, pp. 151–2), or on public funding and private foundations, or bring about a suitable change in our economic system.

Changing the existing economic system logically requires a refusal to purchase products in retail chains, doing without mass consumer goods (almost all processed food, clothing, furniture, electric appliances, cars, alcoholic beverages, cigarettes, and much more), as well as transport and all of the attendant packaging. Instead, people would have to support the retail trade and small local producers. This would also require shouldering the financial burdens of all these changes and finding and convincing a politically effective number of like-minded people.

To exclude existing industrial corporations from using genetic engineering without radically changing the global economic structure at the same time would simply mean supporting the creation of new industrial corporations at the expense of the old ones.

We, the consumers in industrialized nations, damage both the environment and the developing countries – at least indirectly through our lifestyle – and not the industrial corporations in themselves that we, as is often flippantly implied, would have nothing to do with. In this context I would once again like to refer to the previous two chapters as well as the following one, in which this question is discussed a number of times.

Previous experience with one of the first transgenic crops (insect resistant cotton) should prove to be an especially convincing example, as in this case small farmers and environmental protection in developing countries profited more than the seed producers (p. 137).

Will "terminator technology" be used to prevent the unlicensed spreading of seeds in commercial use?

The colloquially used term "terminator technology" (scientifically known as "genetic use of restriction technology," or GURT) refers to a genetically engineered mechanism that causes second generation (harvested) seeds to be sterile, i.e. they cannot be used for future planting. This technology is not yet commercially available and – partly because of the activities of environmental organizations and several large seed producers – placed under an international moratorium. This moratorium, which prohibits the commercial use of GURT, was last extended in April 2006 by the 8th Conference of the Parties of the Convention on Biological Diversity (CBD).

On the one hand GURT is intended to protect seed producers from the unlicensed use of a variety that they developed at great expense, and on the other hand (for ecological or other reasons) to prevent an uncontrolled and undesirable dissemination. It is nevertheless controversial because many small farmers whose existences are already threatened, and who are dependent on self-produced seed because of a lack of money, could be negatively affected by it. Neither the methodological development nor the biological testing is at a stage that would allow for the approval of commercial use in the foreseeable future.

Doesn't the creation of herbicide-tolerant plants through genetic engineering actually increase the use of herbicides instead of reducing it?

Farmers often take advantage of "package deals," which offer herbicide-tolerant plants together with an accompanying herbicide. The greatly increased herbicide tolerance of these crops would allow them to apply more of the herbicide. In doing so they would kill more weeds, but also pollute the environment to a much greater extent.

The intention, however, is just the opposite, and experience thus far has confirmed this impressively. Wherever transgenic herbicide-tolerant plants have been cultivated, herbicide use per unit of area has been considerably reduced. In addition, less selective herbicides and more non-selective herbicides are used which are less harmful to the environment and can be used in smaller quantities. No farmer would use more pesticides than absolutely necessary, for economic reasons alone.

Wherever the use of herbicides is unavoidable, the primary objective must be to reduce the environmental impact through the application of either smaller quantities or less ecologically harmful chemicals (or both). The contribution that genetic engineering can make in this regard has been discussed above (p. 138).

Can food from genetically modified plants cause allergies?

Almost any type of food can cause allergies in certain persons. In most cases, however, only the allergic potential is known, but not the responsible substance. In principle, it is possible to transfer an allergy-causing factor with every new combination of genes – whether through conventional breeding or genetic engineering. It is not genetic engineering as such, but a genetically programmed substance that causes some people to suffer an allergic reaction.

Allergies to plants or plant products that were obtained through conventional breeding can be caused to the same extent by food that contains the same ingredients as a result of genetic engineering. If it is known that the substance in question (often a protein) causes allergic reactions in sensitive people, then the product should be labeled accordingly – exactly like the conventionally bred plant from which the gene was isolated.

It should be emphasized, however, that genetic engineering can also be used to remove an allergy-causing substance.

Can resistance genes that were often used as markers for a successful gene transfer contribute to the spread of resistance to antibiotics?

This possibility cannot be completely ruled out, and therefore a mechanism for self-destruction of the resistance gene subsequent to the gene transfer was added some time ago. This problem mostly concerned the resistance genes for the antibiotics kanamycin and neomycin, which are not commonly used for medical treatment anymore. Besides, intestinal bacteria in healthy people already contain resistance genes that are often found in bacteria and are ingested with food.

This question is no longer valid, however, as these markers are no longer used.

What happens to the additional gene when genetically modified food is consumed or a transgenic plant decomposes?

The first of these two questions is asked surprisingly often and is easy to answer: Our entire plant and animal diet contains billions of genes that are broken down into their basic components in our stomach and intestines and either reutilized in this form by our bodies or further broken down and partly excreted as uric acid. This also applies to the genes that were transferred through genetic engineering.

The question about the process of decomposition in the environment has been less clearly answered to date. Plants and their individual parts in the soil, including their genes, are broken down partially or completely by small animals, fungi, and bacteria and converted into nutrient-rich humus. According to what is currently known, however, it cannot be ruled out that under certain conditions intact genes or parts of them may be preserved for short or even long periods of time. However, because the genes transferred by genetic engineering are generally of natural origin, they share the fate of genes from all other organisms when in the soil.

Will genetic engineering promote a reduction in the diversity of our most important crops?
A reduction in diversity due to the mass cultivation of food and forage crops is indeed a problem that, in principle, could be reinforced through the use of transgenic plants. However, biological constraints, supported by practical experience, would indicate the opposite.

On the one hand, varieties that are adapted to different local conditions are required. Transgenic traits that are developed in prototypes thus have to be crossed into suitable varieties just like other desired breeding results. I have already described the broad breeding effort required with Golden Rice in order to provide the necessary cultivar diversity for different growing areas.

The possible ecological and economic disadvantages of a greatly reduced diversity of varieties were apparent already before the emergence of genetic engineering, especially in connection with the Green Revolution. A sustainable, productive, and environmentally friendly form of agriculture is not conceivable without a great cultivar and species diversity of crops (p. 221). This applies to all products of plant breeding, with or without genetic engineering.

Will an increased supply of food provided through plant genetic engineering promote population growth and thus prevent its cessation?
As early as 1798 Thomas Robert Malthus formulated his hypothesis (which is often incompletely cited and partially misquoted) that population growth is directly dependent on the supply of food. This hypothesis has often been disproved since then, even if under certain circumstances it may be accurate, and the blanket judgment of Malthus from some quarters certainly did him an injustice.

The current situation clearly shows how little cause there is for these types of fears. The opposite may actually be true: the largest population growth nowadays is found in areas experiencing famine, while in countries with sufficient amounts of easily accessible food the population figures are stable or even declining.

Self-imposed Rules and Subsequent Laws

Genetic engineering began with the realization that methods in molecular biology would permit the genetic modification of living organisms. The first attempts were confined to bacteria. As this new possibility became evident the scientists working in this field took the initiative and responsibility and drew up guidelines and restrictions under which all work in molecular biology and genetic engineering has been carried out since then. Among the restrictions are the use of special laboratory strains of bacteria that are not capable of surviving in natural environments (p. 132) and work in controlled areas. These areas are divided into different levels of safety depending on the type of organism. The high-risk level of containment is for experiments with dangerous pathogens affecting higher animals and humans. Such work is only carried out in a few laboratories worldwide.

These guidelines were introduced at a molecular biology conference in the United States in 1975 and declared obligatory worldwide. At first they were voluntarily adhered to by scientists until national laws and guidelines were formally adopted. Typically, they closely followed the self-imposed rules which, for reasons of caution, were stricter than deemed necessary at that time. After years of experience some parts of these laws were relaxed. The resulting new version is now in force in a majority of countries and has proved suitable in many years of practice since then.

Up to now there have been no known cases in which genetic engineering as such has led to any apparent danger for humans or the environment.

Science and the General Public

Despite all the temporary regresses the worldwide advancement of democratic political systems as a consequence of the individual emancipation of people is among the radical changes that have occurred since the Enlightenment. The result has been a general public which represents the civic community, as the "broad mass" of the population, and is equipped with corresponding rights, e.g. a comprehensive right to information about everything that affects the state and its resources.

This right to information also extends to publicly and (to a certain extent) privately funded scientific institutions and projects. There are good as well as important reasons for this. Today an individual scientist can develop knowledge or products that have far-reaching effects. Any potentially affected person therefore has the right to be informed. No one, however, is obliged to be informed, but everyone nevertheless has a direct or indirect right of participation in fundamental decision making – including scientific issues – for instance through elections, memberships in associations, or donations to lobby groups. This is a serious unsolved problem which, in the case of genetic engineering, has become especially apparent. The layperson exercises his right to be informed, if at all, almost exclusively through the mass media, i.e. television, internet, radio, newspapers, and magazines, and to a much lesser extent through popular science publications. There are serious shortcomings in this deficit, which are only partially caused by science itself:

- Many scientists are either not prepared to provide information, largely because of the considerable amount of time involved and the small chances of success, or they are not properly trained to do so;
- funding is easier to obtain for research than for presenting its results in a generally comprehensible fashion;
- scientific information can only be properly communicated directly (not indirectly using paraphrasing) and thus requires thorough and sober explanations to which laypersons are unaccustomed;
- many laypersons are either uninterested or only poorly and partially interested in this type of information;
- today's type of media consumption has become so sensationalist that well-balanced, neutral, and objective communication of scientific information is difficult, if not impossible;
- sensationalist falsification is often greatly reinforced through incomplete and hasty investigation;
- the common use of trick shots as a means of style, even in documentary films, has made it very difficult to distinguish real (science) from phony (fiction).

This stresses the dire need of improvement of all three parts of the information chain (science, media, and the general public). The barriers between each of these parts can only be removed by intensifying the efforts and improving the quality of the overall flow of information.

Many scientists are not prepared to play their part as a source of information as long as the results are factually incorrect or sensationalist and fear-mongering interpretations – as are the majority of the depictions I have seen about genetic engineering on television and radio, or in newspapers and magazines. On the other hand, many journalists (the exceptions to this rule are all the more remarkable!) obviously have the problem that their chances of getting ahead will be negatively affected if they write factually correct reports that are considered boring by viewers, listeners, or readers. Those who are insufficiently informed rightly complain about the lack of dependable and accurate information, but they seldom notice just how much they themselves are responsible for this grievance due to their behavior as uncritical consumers seeking excitement and entertainment.

The ethical evaluation of genetic engineering requires responsibility at every level. Even if scientists and the media have to improve the flow of information, individual consumers are responsible for the way they acquire and digest information, as well as the way they draw their conclusions and make judgments.

Scientists have the greatest responsibility of all. This will remain without consequences, however, if there is no corresponding willingness to impartially integrate their findings into everyone's common responsibility. The pressing problem of effectively protecting the environment while simultaneously producing enough food for everyone will neither be achieved by scare tactics nor by glossing over the facts.

Relative Criteria

There is no absolute scale for ethical evaluations. The only possible alternative, the normative definition of a relative scale, is all the more difficult the more open a question of evaluation is; that is, the more divided the opinions are. "You should not kill" is an order that most people would agree with. It refers to all people, and probably in its original meaning particularly to every individual as the potential victim who therefore needs to be protected. It reveals the relativity of the scale in a number of ways: the point of reference is the human being, and primarily one's self. Even this scale becomes relativized in a borderline case to the point that, except for suicide and killing in self-defense or an emergency, killing in a war is even demanded.

The killing of animals that belonged to others was considered *property* damage until recently. This offence has now been legally adjusted to become more specific. And yet animals, provided certain animal protection restrictions are fulfilled, can still be killed to provide food or for research purposes. Most animals may even be killed heedlessly or intentionally, and this is not forbidden as long as they are not specifically protected by general laws of conservation or as endangered species. This also applies to plants and microorganisms, although the restrictions are even less stringent.

The ban on killing is a ban on doing the wrong thing, or an indirect order to do what is right. Many of our ethically motivated patterns of behavior are expressed in our laws as clear formulations of bans instead of orders, for example not to steal but instead to respect the property of others, or not to go through a red light, but a green one instead. The vastly different kinds and severities of penalties that are threatened in different cultures indicate the relativity of scales of value.

Relative scales have to be applied to genetic engineering as well. This is especially apparent from the fact that in numerous countries with comparable research activities, field trials and the cultivation of genetically modified organisms are regulated very differently and are also evaluated differently by the public. Valid norms must nonetheless be determined early enough and applied as uniformly as possible on an international scale. The following ethical and biological aspects could serve as a scale.

- From an ethical point of view the human germline has to be protected – without exceptions for now (p. 182) – from any genetic engineering intervention. Pragmatic principles could be developed for all other organisms:
  - Genetic engineering can be applied with such organisms that are also bred with other methods, as long as this offers more advantages than disadvantages for the environment, human nutrition, and human health.
  - A normative decision about the goals and limits of human intervention in the evolution of organisms by any method is urgently needed in view of the increasing possibilities of new breeding techniques (cell culture technology, artificial insemination, cloning, and genetic engineering) as well as urgent overriding problems (the environment, human nutrition, and health).
- To the extent that genetic engineering is affected by these types of decisions, three levels of genetic modification can be distinguished:
  1. The transfer, removal, activation, or inactivation of unmodified genes which could also be transferred or modified in their activity levels with conventional methods;
  2. modifications of species-specific genes which can only be carried out with genetic engineering methods;
  3. modifications which can only be carried out with genetic engineering methods, using either foreign or synthetic genes, or parts thereof.
- In addition, different groups of organisms can be distinguished according to the risk potential of genetic modifications; in the following order from negligible to high:
  1. Organisms that cannot survive in a natural environment, e.g. "laboratory strains" of bacteria;

2. Organisms that either cannot survive – or can only survive to a certain extent – without human cultivation in a natural environment, for instance many of our most important food plants and animals, several ornamental plants, and pets;

3. All other organisms excluding:

4. Pathogens of all organisms with the exception of those affecting humans;

5. Pathogens that affect humans.

Further distinctions are possible, but are unnecessary at the present stage of development and in our context. It may have already become sufficiently clear that ethical evaluations cannot be derived on a purely theoretical basis, i.e. without reference to practical implications, and therefore cannot be completely unequivocal. With this in mind, I will make some suggestions for a practical approach in the final chapter.

Summary

Ethical scales of value are relative and based on the defini-tion of goals. The decisive criterion for the ethical evalua-tion of plant genetic engineering is the comparison of an increased intervention in the evolution of food plants (e.g. by crossing species boundaries) with an ecological disas-ter caused by the overuse of our biosphere, primarily to produce enough food for the human population.

Although genetic engineering is still in an early phase of its practical application, it has clearly proven its use-fulness in the areas of human health (medical research and the production of pharmaceuticals) and agriculture (increased yields, lower costs and reductions in environ-mental impacts). Based on experience to date, and *if used properly*, genetic engineering should pose no danger to humans or the environment. Misgivings to the contrary without factual substantiation are an expression of a lack of global responsibility and the result of a sensationalist or ideological falsification of the intentions and goals of genetic engineering. An unbiased evaluation of the oppor-tunities and risks of genetic engineering presupposes an independent ability to judge on the basis of appropriate fundamental knowledge and requires improved communi-cation between science and the general public.

8 Basic Prerequisites for Securing Human Nourishment

The Earth could now provide enough food for six or seven billion people, and presumably even more. The fact that almost one billion people are going hungry, and that many of them are even starving to death, is not because of a lack of food. It is due to a lack of solidarity and sharing. Those who are hungry are so desperately poor that they even lack the means to acquire a bare minimum of food. Regardless of this situation, however, considerable corrections in the current use of available resources are essential in order to secure a future source of food for everyone.

The future is always open. Forecasts of the future are no more than assumptions of probability about the development of present trends and foreseeable changes. Despite their restricted significance, they nonetheless serve as valuable guidelines for preventive measures. The often-predicted growth in population to eight or even ten billion people within the next few decades can only be understood as an urgent warning and as a call for immediate action.

As in the preceding chapters, I will forego the use of detailed numerical data as much as possible here as well. What counts is the way this challenge is dealt with and not absolute numbers, which can always be contested no matter how thorough they may be. Those readers who are interested in details will find data and extensive references in three thorough and yet highly readable treatises which I will refer to in greater scope: *Outgrowing the Earth. The Food Security Challenge in an Age of Falling Water Tables and Rising Temperatures* by Lester R. Brown; *The Doubly Green Revolution. Food for all in the 21st Century* by Gordon Conway; and *Feeding the Ten Billion. Plants and Population Growth* by Lloyd T. Evans.

In addition to their own research, all three authors base their books mainly on assessments and prognoses made by the World Bank's International Food Policy Institute (IFPRI), the United Nation's Food and Agriculture Organization (FAO), as well as other publicly available sources, which are widely quoted. These and other references cited in this chapter are listed at the end of the book.

The Global Perspective

I have already pointed out the exceptional conditions of agricultural productivity in Europe (p. 176). A comparison of the yield per hectare in several of the world's most important wheat growing areas illustrates this particularly well. In 2002, for instance, France's average yield per hectare was approximately two and a half times as high as that in the United States, and more than three times as high as that in Argentina, Canada, Australia, or Russia.

We owe this exceptional position, particularly in Western European countries, to the confluence of three complementary factors: 1. the warm Gulf Stream, which provides a balanced climate with high amounts of precipitation and relatively mild winter and summer temperatures compared to other regions in this geographic latitude; 2. long periods of daylight during the growing and ripening periods in the summer; and 3. fertile humus-rich soils.

A look at both of the world's most densely populated regions, Asia and Africa, makes this difference very apparent. Great contrasts between zones with lush vegetation and huge, literally bone-dry deserts are aggravated by predominantly nutrient-poor soils, nearly constant periods of daylight near the equator, and large temperature differences between hot dry summers and very cold winters in areas far from the equator. And the forecasts are particularly unfavorable for these parts of the world which are already overpopulated: the highest population growth, the biggest poverty problems, a major lack of food and water, and a rapid expansion of deserts.

Population Growth

Even if absolute values for estimates of population growth differ from one another considerably and are increasingly being revised downwards, most predictions foresee approximately nine billion people by the year 2050. A continuation of current trends is implied. According to these predictions, growth will occur almost exclusively in developing countries, especially in Asia and Africa.

The highest relative growth among the twenty most populous countries (with a doubling of the population in each case) within the next fifty years is predicted to occur in Pakistan, Nigeria, and Ethiopia. Even stronger growth, which will lead to populations that are four or five times what they are now, is predicted for countries like Uganda, The Democratic Republic of Congo, and Yemen, thus putting them into the "Top 20."

And yet, the question about how this will be possible remains unanswered. According to the *Human Development Report 2005* every one of these six countries is already in the lowest part (the last quarter) of the "Human Development Index." They all have great problems with the supply of food and water, with poverty and a lack of education, as well as border, tribal, and religious conflicts which include civil wars, expulsions, and the mass exodus of starving ethnic groups. And it is exactly these countries that are losing large areas of their arable fields and pastures through erosion and desertification (pp. 217 and 222).

India is predicted to have the greatest absolute population growth of all: from a little more than a billion people to one and a half billion. In 2050 India would then be ahead of China as the most populous country in the world. Once again the question arises as to how this type of jump should be dealt with. Even today, India's population density is only slightly less than that of the Netherlands, Europe's most densely populated country. The Ganges River barely flows to its confluence with the Brahmaputra River, the water table is sinking dramatically in most places, and rice and wheat yields have stagnated in the last ten years. More than half of India's population now lives below the poverty level, one quarter is malnourished and many people are starving.

Having more people not only means a greater demand for food, but for living space and other resources as well. Besides a sufficient quality and quantity of food, every additional person requires water to drink and for other basic needs, a place to live, different forms of directly or indirectly consumed energy, a share of transport routes, education, and a job with an adequate income. All people produce waste and attempt to become prosperous, avoiding poverty and threats to their existence.

Every one of these needs is satisfied at the cost of valuable agricultural land and great amounts of water and energy, all of which are needed directly or indirectly for the production and processing of food. Almost all human settlement areas, from farms to large cities, are founded and developed on land which is especially fertile and suitable for agriculture.

In addition, there is the trend over decades of continuously growing cities with their dense residential neighborhoods and all sorts of consequential symptoms such as waste, hygiene, and traffic problems, social conflicts and, not least of all, the danger of the development and dissemination of infectious diseases. Conditions in the poor sections of Europe's major cities are luxurious in comparison with the huge slums and favelas of African, Asian, or Latin American mega-cities such as Lagos, Calcutta, São Paulo, and many others.

The true horror of poverty and hunger can probably only be understood when looking directly into the eyes of those who suffer so tremendously: the desperately hungry, begging, and uncared-for cripples in the streets of a huge Indian city, or the apathetic Indios in the South American Andes who squat next to open sewers trying to still their hunger by chewing coca leaves.

Poverty and Wealth

The conflict-laden, sorrowful, and checkered history of poverty and wealth is presumably as old as the cultural history of humankind. Jared Diamond has impressively described this in his bestseller *Guns, Gems, and Steel*. Today, 10% of the world's population disposes of 54% of its income, while 40% live on less than two dollars a day (and many of them on even less than one dollar a day) and dispose of approximately 5% of the world's income (Fig. 32). According to the *Human Development Report 2005* the world's wealthiest 500 individuals have a combined income greater than the poorest 416 million people.

The gap between rich and poor is steadily growing. I have

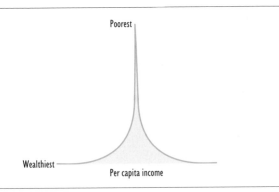

Figure 32 Distribution curve of world per capita income (in 2000) by the
          wealthiest (bottom) and the poorest (top)

already pointed out the serious consequences that malnutrition has for the poor inhabitants of developing countries in the context of Golden Rice and the objectives of several large humanitarian foundations (pp. 149ff.). Despite all the recognition that such initiatives deserve, however, improved access to high-quality food alone cannot solve the problem of mass poverty in developing countries.

The big contrast between rich and poor is not only a symbol of the long way that the cultural development of the "civilized world" still has to go. It also very clearly indicates the size of the problem. Apart from the catastrophe of nearly a billion people going hungry or starving – often accompanied by wars, mass flight, expulsions, and massacres – we are also faced in a very direct way with the consequences of continuing population growth in the famine-stricken areas of a demographically, economically, and politically closely linked world.

For a better understanding of this statement let us return once again to the example of India and assume – despite all doubts – that the population grows to 1.5 billion people within the next 50 years. Let us also assume that the United Nation's seemingly utopian goal of reducing the number of people who suffer from hunger by half by 2015 was completely or at least partially achieved. And finally, for population development in the coming decades, let us further assume that general conditions similar to those in the recent past continue to prevail and thus substantiate the reliability of the predictions. If this were the case, we would be faced with a situation whose global consequences would vastly exceed recent developments in China.

In China during the period of forced collectivization and industrialization between 1959 and 1961 an estimated 30 million people died of starvation. Since then the supply of food has been one of the priority issues of every Chinese government. By 1999 the production of rice, corn, and wheat had increased fourfold and China temporarily became an exporter of these crops. This trend has since been reversed, partially as a result of increasing problems of irrigation in the northern wheat growing areas (p. 223). Within a few years China went from being self-sufficient to being the world's greatest importer of wheat and soy.

The profits China earns from its exports make the importation of food possible, as well as the importation of oil, steel, precious metals, and other goods for the rapid economic, civil, and military development of the country. Those who have kept an eye on the building booms in the centers of the big cities and the many newly developed suburbs with their comfortable townhouses and single-family houses, the ever-present construction of roads and highways, and the rapidly increasing automobile and air traffic in the last few years will understand the following counterarguments.

The currently more than 25 million cars in China require

about 500,000 hectares of roads and parking lots. If used for agricultural purposes, this amount of land would feed several million people. A further per capita increase in the motorization of the Chinese population up to the levels of present-day Japan would, according to Lester Brown's calculations in *Outgrowing the Earth*, correspond to about two-thirds of the entire area now used in China to cultivate rice. Basically the same applies to the expansion of urban development with its corresponding utilization of land, water, and energy.

The number of poor and starving people in China has gone down as the prosperity of the upper and middle income groups has rapidly increased. With this increase in prosperity, however, the demand for higher quality food has also risen: vegetables, fruit, fish, and meat, the latter with a corresponding use of forage crops at the cost of food crops – thus disadvantaging the production of basic foodstuffs (p. 230).

If this trend continues and China's rising prosperity causes the shortages and thus prices for food and feed to balloon like they have for steel and oil, then this will not be without consequences for the rest of the world. It will become especially difficult for the projected half billion additional Indians, not to mention the further 2.5 billion people that will allegedly be born almost exclusively in the poorest developing countries.

The situation appears to be paradoxical: Poverty and scarcity promote population growth – their elimination impairs food production, thus increasing scarcity. The fictional example of a level of motorization in China equal to that of Japan indicates the only conceivable solution:

> The elimination of poverty as a source of population growth
> is the top priority. An inevitable consequence, however, will
> be a major change in lifestyle in the industrialized countries,

with prosperity and the quality of life being based on such precious, long ignored values as the preservation of a human life-supporting biosphere and global solidarity.

The Green Revolution

The fact that the number of starving and malnourished people is not substantially greater than it is, despite the extremely precipitous growth of the world's population in the recent past (Fig. 1, p. 7), is due to a simultaneous and unique leap in agricultural productivity: the "Green Revolution."

The Green Revolution was the result of a concerted effort of agricultural research and practice, humanitarian foundations, development aid, and government programs in those countries that received help. The common goal was the fight against hunger and poverty. The starting point in 1943 was a joint project of the Rockefeller Foundation and the Mexican Ministry of Agriculture, aimed at improving corn and wheat varieties for cultivation in Mexico.

Through the successful adaptation of North American varieties to local conditions in Mexico the country became independent of corn imports within a few years. Similar successes were soon achieved with new varieties of wheat. In both cases, in addition to breeding, more efficient methods of cultivation played an important role, especially the intensification of fertilization, pest management, and irrigation.

The decisive breakthrough with wheat, however, was achieved through the use of a dwarf variety that had been bred in Japan. This variety had two qualities which complemented each other and since revolutionized the cultivation of wheat around the world: higher yields of grain at the cost of stalk length, and increased stability of the short-stalked varieties under unfavorable weather conditions.

Further breeding improvements included: increased disease resistance, reduced dependence on the amount of daylight and other environmental factors, efficient utilization of fertilizer, and adaptation to previously unsuited locations. Within a short period of time the successes and improvements in the supply of food in numerous developing countries were so impressive that the initiator and founding director of the International Maize and Wheat Research Center (*Centro International de Mejoramiento de Maíz y Trigo, or* CIMMYT) in Mexico City, Norman Borlaug, was awarded the Nobel Peace Prize in 1970.

An equally rapid development of rice followed this pioneering step. Once again the use of dwarf varieties played a significant role.

A special feature of rice is the short generation time, especially in warm growing areas. Two or even three harvests per year are possible with early-maturing and seasonally independent varieties. Breeding efforts have been undertaken to further improve these traits. If the various resistance and tolerance characteristics of rice, its efficient utilization of nutrients, and its adaptability to local conditions – particularly to different forms of irrigation – are also taken into account, then the breadth of diversity of rice cultivars for an equally diverse number of growing conditions and household as well as industrial uses becomes apparent.

In order to achieve rapid distribution of these new high-yielding varieties they were first given to farmers in several developing countries free of charge, among others the Philippines. A short time later combined packages of seed, fertilizer, and pesticides were put together in the proper quantities. In this manner the farmers, who had no experience with the new methods of cultivation, were able to familiarize themselves with these innovations.

The general result of the Green Revolution was a historically unique jump in agricultural productivity. The largest yield increases of all three main food sources – wheat, rice, and corn – were achieved coincident with the most precipitous growth in the human population during the second half of the 20th century (p. 8). Between 1970 and 1995, toward the end of the shortest doubling period of the population ever, the number of people suffering from hunger actually fell slightly instead of rising proportionally.

Several large humanitarian foundations contributed significantly to this success in addition to numerous government aid programs organized by industrialized countries and the complementary investment programs of the developing countries. With the support of the Rockefeller and Ford Foundations a series of international research institutes were founded after the CIMMYT, among them the International Rice Research Institute (IRRI) in the Philippine capital, Manila. This institute played an essential part in the rapid increase of rice yields and is presently involved in the development of Golden Rice (p. 152).

In addition to the Green Revolution's great successes, there have also been problems associated with it. In two of the regions most threatened by problems of hunger, South Asia and Sub-Saharan Africa, particularly poor inhabitants were either barely affected by the improvements or even put at a disadvantage. A new gap opened up within the class of the socially underprivileged: the position of the 'poorest of the poor', which already represented the largest proportion of starving people, became even more precarious.

Ecological problems were also aggravated by the rapid

intensification of fertilization, pesticide use, and irrigation. Especially at the beginning of the Green Revolution, when small farmers had no experience with the new cultivation techniques, soils and water were often polluted by the excessive application of fertilizers and pesticides. In addition, there was an overuse of water resources, with some bodies of water completely drying up (p. 223), and a spread of plant diseases and pest insects because of the mass cultivation of high-yielding varieties. This in turn led to further increases in the application of environmentally damaging pesticides.

On the other hand, the fact remains that in large parts of Asia a doubling of cereal production was achieved while the area under cultivation only increased by 4%. For the first time in the history of humankind the production of food was able to keep pace with massive population growth without requiring a corresponding growth in agriculturally used areas.

This type of increase in productivity cannot, however, be continued any longer with existing means – neither in Asia nor anywhere else. The Green Revolution itself needs to be revolutionized to become a Doubly Green Revolution.

Vision of a Doubly Green Revolution

The "Doubly Green Revolution" is an expression coined by the Consultative Group on International Agricultural Research (CGIAR) under the direction of Gordon Conway, the author of *The Doubly Green Revolution*. It stands for the conception of a second type of Green Revolution that asks for both a more efficient and yet ecologically considerate form of agriculture and a complementary revolution in food production.

The consultative group assumes that a secure future for

human nourishment is fundamentally possible, but not without drastic changes in the present practice. For this to occur they have put forward three indispensable demands:

1. Another significant increase in agricultural productivity, which has often stagnated or even declined since the end of the Green Revolution's large increases around 1990.
2. A strict observance of sustainability, i.e. the production of food without causing long-term damage to the environment.
3. Secure access to a sufficient amount and quality of food for all people.

To achieve this they have made a series of concrete recommendations. The most important are:

- analyzing and eliminating the reasons for decreasing yields with the intensive and one-sided cultivation of cereals;
- the application of both conventional and genetic engineering methods to develop new cultivars that allow for higher yields while requiring less care, and have an increased resistance or tolerance of environmental stress;
- the development of integrated, environmentally friendly programs for fertilization and pest management;
- the development and use of efficient methods of irrigation, water conservation, protection of water resources, and water quality management;
- the reduced production of greenhouse gases (especially methane) and nitrogen oxides in agriculture (p. 217);
- the intensification of ecosystem research, particularly in ecologically sensitive areas;
- the development of alternatives to slash-and-burn land clearing and shifting cultivation on unproductive soils;

- the creation of jobs in the processing and distribution of foodstuffs;
- the creation of jobs and sources of income in the sustainable management of forests, fishing grounds, and other natural resources.

The entire list is substantially longer and includes numerous specific measures for the solution of regional or otherwise restricted problems. The urgent need for improved education and professional training, medical care, instruction about proper nutrition, and training in modern agricultural techniques in rural areas of developing countries is emphasized in particular.

In essence, all of these recommendations are aimed at securing "Food for All in the Twenty-First Century" (as the book's subheading concisely formulates) and opening up new approaches to agricultural production after the world's biological limits have become so obvious, and in many cases have been far exceeded.

The Biological Limits of Agricultural Productivity

Agricultural productivity is limited by two different types of biological constraint:

1. the capacity of the biosphere to withstand interference with the stability and dynamic development of ecosystems, and
2. the physiological efficiency of organisms or individual organs that are consumed as food.

I have already discussed the limits of interfering with individual ecosystems (pp. 58ff.). Endangering the biosphere as a whole is the subject of the following sections. The limits of physiological efficiency have also been mentioned several times, especially in connection with the breeding emphasis on particular organs in various Solanaceae and Brassicaceae species (p. 95ff.), as well as in connection with the anticipated, though somewhat questionable increase in photosynthetic efficiency (p. 156).

Our most important sources of food, the various cereal species, are particularly good examples of the limits of physiological efficiency. Their special position as basic foodstuffs is, among other specific features, due to two spontaneous mutations (p. 108ff.), i.e. genetically fixed modifications that have lastingly determined their evolution as crops.

The first and most important of these mutations marked the beginning of the Neolithic Revolution. It involved the change from brittle to tough ears and significantly influenced the breeding history of all agriculturally used cereals (pp. 108–9). The second mutation, shortening the stalk length in favor of larger ears (and thus increased yields), occurred much more recently, and with wheat and rice was one of the fundamental elements of the Green Revolution.

Both mutations are extremely disadvantageous in terms of survival of the species, as they impair the ability to compete under natural reproductive conditions. The brittleness of the ear is a prerequisite for seed dissemination as it has developed over the course of evolution. The natural stalk length was also the result of a long-term evolutionary adaptation to existing living conditions (capturing light, wind pollination, etc.). Both mutations are highly advantageous for the agricultural conditions created by humans, but in the wild, except for a few special situations, would lead to the extinction of the affected individuals.

Spontaneous mutations that have such far-reaching consequences on human nutrition are extremely rare and have biological as well as practical limits. On the one hand, there is an inherent biological limit up to which a plant (or any other organism) will tolerate the reprogramming of its exquisitely balanced metabolism and anatomical structure. On the other hand, agricultural practice has to observe the biosphere's limits of tolerance for human cultivation and farming methods.

Most of today's high-yielding varieties have to a great extent already reached the biological limits of agricultural yields. The future breeding goals with most of our cereal, vegetable, fruit, and potato cultivars will primarily be concerned with improving their overall quality, resistance, and other characteristics, and much less with further increases in yield.

The different types of vegetables illustrated in Figs. 16 and 17 (color plates II and III) are not the only evidence of these constraints. There is also the fact that with today's cereals the "yield index," i.e. the relative share of harvested kernels in comparison to the plant's entire dry weight, is already more than 50%. Because healthy and functioning roots, stalks, and leaves are essential to the production of kernels, this value, which is comparable to that of the vegetables depicted, can no longer be substantially increased.

Insofar as yield can be further improved at all through genetic modifications (any kind of breeding), this will probably occur with those few crops that have not already been bred for extreme efficiency and diverse conditions of cultivation despite their existing potential. Quinoa and Amaranth, for instance, are two old South American crops that in many parts of Europe have so far been largely confined to health food and fair trade shops.

The biosphere's tolerance limit, which is difficult to define, has also been mentioned several times and will continue to play an important role in this book. Hence, I will limit myself to a few fundamental comments at this point. To begin with, however, a definition of the concept of "the biosphere's tolerance limit" is needed: In our context of sustainable production of food, this is the extent of interference which the Earth's biosphere will tolerate without long-term damage to the conditions for human life.

It is not just a matter of merely preserving any type of biosphere as such. It is a matter of preserving a biosphere that will provide seven billion or more human beings with a suitable place to live and a sufficient amount of food.

One of the many recent examples of large-scale and perhaps irreversible violation of a limit in this sense was the transformation of gigantic areas of the Kazakh Steppe in the former Soviet Union (now Kazakhstan) into farmland. These areas were suitable for growing wheat only for a short period of time and are now predominantly unplanted and desolate. In the meantime, wind erosion and dust storms have turned a major portion of the land into deserts that are now useless for either agriculture or grazing. Even where the cultivation of wheat is still possible, the yield per hectare is far below the world's average. The biosphere will need a long time to close these wounds – provided they are breached no further.

Instead of expanding unsuited areas for agricultural purposes, future food production must concentrate on areas that will remain fertile for an extended period of time. This includes, wherever possible, the multiple use of land through two or three annual yields, and a continuous increase in efficiency through breeding as well as improved methods of cultivation, storage, and distribution of the end product. There is much room for improvement in all of these areas, especially in developing countries.

Multiple use requires suitable conditions of cultivation as well as varieties which grow and mature quickly. The best example is rice farming in water-rich, climatically favorable areas where up to three harvests per year can be obtained for an extended period of time. For most other field crops this can more likely be achieved by crop rotation, if possible including a legume to reduce nitrogen fertilization, e.g. by alternating corn with soy. Another method, which is particularly common among small farmers who grow their own food in developing countries, consists of mixed cultivation of different species. This was already practiced successfully by the ancient Greeks and Romans, for instance using olives, grapes, and wheat.

The greatest potential for increased yields, however, lies in tolerance and resistance breeding and in the improvement of farming methods, storage, and distribution. In warm and humid climates in tropical and subtropical regions up to half, and in extreme cases even more, of the potential yield is lost to pre- and post-harvest diseases and pests, and to a lack of proper infrastructure. These losses can and must be significantly reduced.

One of the keys to securing human sustenance lies in this area, particularly if combined with continued breeding efforts for quality improvements. Two essential conditions must nevertheless be met:

- adverse effects to the climate and environment must not be allowed to exceed the biosphere's tolerance limits, and
- political measures must provide adequate research, development, and educational programs, improved social, medical, and economic conditions, as well as the necessary infrastructure (pp. 236ff.).

Weather, Climate, and Environment

We are used to thinking about sunshine and warmth as "good" weather and precipitation as "bad." In agriculture other criteria apply. Here the plant's varying needs during the different stages of development from germination to the maturation of leaves, tubers, beets, or fruit are decisive. Greatly simplified, this means: moisture and warmth during growth, sun and warmth for ripening, and favorable conditions for sowing and harvesting.

The more reliably these conditions are met, and the less often they are interrupted by storms or other hazards, the more reliable the expected yield will be. The prevailing weather and its stability or instability are determining factors in this regard. In this series Mojib Latif describes this in more detail in *Climate Change: The Point of No Return*.

The threat of climate change has been a much-discussed topic for some years now. Obvious reasons are the rapidly increasing average annual temperatures, melting glaciers, snow fields, and polar ice caps, as well as the regular occurrence of "100-year events", such as extremely intense rainstorms and flooding, exceedingly hot and dry summers, particularly fierce and destructive cyclones, etc.

This affects food production in two ways. On the one hand, all crops and cultivars have been adapted to particular growing areas and are thus dependent on the respective climatic and weather conditions. On the other hand, agriculture itself is largely involved in the production of greenhouse gases and the elimination of climate-stabilizing biotopes, especially the tropical rainforests and other extensive forest areas (Fig. 33).

The greenhouse gases produced by agriculture are mainly methane and carbon dioxide. In addition, nitrogenous gases that act as acidifiers and catalysts for chemical reactions are released into the atmosphere. These gases are formed in great amounts through slash-and-burn methods of clearing land as well as the burning of wood, grass, and straw. The amount of carbon dioxide produced in this manner is somewhat less than

Figure 33 Large-scale deforestation of the Amazon Jungle in Mato
Grosso, Brazil

the amount released around the world through the combustion
of fossil fuels – but even here agribusiness is extensively involved.
Large quantities of methane are also formed through biological processes in rice fields and in the stomachs of ruminants.
Approximately the same amounts of nitrogen oxides are set free
from fertilizers as are produced through the practice of slash-
and-burn and other forms of combustion.

All in all, the production of food, including the clearing of
forests and the use of energy, contributes more to the supposed
causes of global warming, and thus to possible large-scale climate
changes, than any other part of the economy. Consequently, this
poses an increasing threat as the population continues to grow.
This major contribution by agriculture to climate change is
further aggravated by its massive interference with the hydrologic balance (pp. 222ff.) as well as large-scale soil erosion and

Figure 34 Desertification at the Kebili Oasis in Tunisia

desertification. Any kind of overuse of farmland and pastures endangers the preservation of the fertile topsoil.

The agricultural sector in Africa and Asia suffers the greatest damage in this regard (Fig. 34). For instance, in Africa's most populous country Nigeria, a total of 100,000 hectares of agricultural and pastureland are lost every year through desertification. Each year several million tons of previously fertile topsoil are blown away by dust storms into the Atlantic Ocean and as far away as the Caribbean and South America.

The situation is similar in China (p. 223), Kazakhstan (p. 214), India, Ethiopia, and numerous other Asian and African countries. The Midwestern United States experienced severe erosion and gigantic dust storms (the Dust Bowl) in the 1930s that reached all the way to Washington, D.C., and New York City. Even in Western Europe, with its favorable climatic conditions, the southeast of Spain has been affected by a persistent drought for several years.

The relationships and feedback mechanisms between weather, climate, the environment, and human intervention are so complex that concrete predictions about long-term regional or global impacts are not possible. What is clear, however, is that a warming of the climate and the large-scale elimination of climate-stabilizing forests and wetlands will have significant effects on agricultural productivity. Every region can be affected – even Western Europe, which has been so fortunate up to now.

Cautionary examples of the loss of productive areas, the irreversibility of large-scale changes, and the sensitivity of the weather, climate and ecosystems to seemingly slight disturbances exist in alarming numbers and in great clarity. It is high time to draw the necessary conclusions.

Species Diversity – Biodiversity – Cultivar Diversity

The importance of biological diversity for the stability of ecosystems and the biosphere as a whole has been discussed previously (pp. 10 and 63ff.). Understanding and respecting the complex ecological relationships is one of the most important prerequisites for securing the long-term supply of human food. These relationships have been thoroughly explained in Josef Reichholf's book in this series *The Demise of Diversity*.

We normally perceive biological diversity as species richness. In fact, it reaches far beyond the immediately visible and comprises the entire spectrum of genetic diversity contained within each species due to the universal phenomenon of genetic variability (p. 93).

The *Diversity of Life* and the *Future of Life* are the most

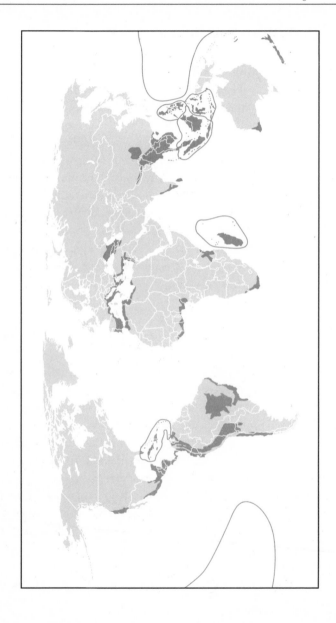

appropriate titles of two complementary bestsellers by Harvard professor and Pulitzer prize-winner Edward O. Wilson, in which he describes with notable urgency the ecological, and (if thoughtfully utilized) the economic and social values of biodiversity. His description of the grave consequences of the progressive destruction of the last few generally intact *biodiversity hotspots* – regions with an exceptional wealth of biological diversity – is particularly impressive.

Most of these biodiversity hotspots are located in tropical or subtropical areas that are particularly threatened by climate change and various forms of economic overuse (Fig. 35). Countless species are being eliminated through the extensive clearing of tropical rainforests as well as the destruction of coral reefs and other species-rich aquatic and wetland biotopes before they can even be "discovered" by humans. Apart from their immense intrinsic value, with every loss of an unknown species there is also an unknown and therefore inestimable loss of ecological stability and adaptability, of genetic resources for breeding, of potential medicines, and of other options for economic use.

The genetic uniformity of a cultivated field of modern high-yielding varieties, e.g. the wheat cultivar in Fig. 3 (p. 11), is the exact opposite of the great genetic diversity of biodiversity hotspots. The extremes of ecological stability are correspondingly far apart. With agricultural monocultures the complete loss of ecological stability has to be compensated for by applying intensive measures of protection and maintenance (p. 73ff.). Reducing the consequential environmental impact to an ecologically acceptable extent is one of the main goals of the Doubly Green Revolution.

Figure 35 Global distribution of biodiversity hotspots

Protecting natural biodiversity has to be coupled with the use of the largest possible species and cultivar diversity in agriculture. This goal can be achieved through several coordinated measures:

- an increase in the diversity and rotation frequency of cultivars in adjacent fields, combined with limited field sizes;
- the mixed cultivation of related cultivars which differ in certain complementary traits, e.g. different types of pathogen resistance to reduce the risk of infections and of the development of new virulent strains (p. 80);
- an increase of species diversity in addition to cultivar diversity, as well as more frequent and coordinated crop rotations;
- the creation and maintenance of biotope corridors, e.g. hedgerows and untreated strips along fields, as well as adequately large networks of connecting passages that allow animals to move undisturbed from one biotope to another.

Water as a Resource

The importance of water and the threats to water resources have been emphasized on several occasions. Both issues are discussed in more detail in Wolfram Mauser's book in this series *Water Resources: Efficient, Sustainable, and Equitable Use.*

On average, agriculture uses almost 70% of all water consumed by humans around the world. (For the production of 1 kg of grains, a wheat, corn, or rice plant requires about 1000 liters, and a coffee tree requires up to 20,000 liters of water per kg of coffee beans!).

The increasing overuse of water – not least because of the

Green Revolution (p. 209) – has led to shortages and the drying up or pollution of many water resources in numerous previously fertile regions. Various large rivers whose once flourishing valleys were the birthplace of the Neolithic Revolution are now heavily polluted and have very little water flowing to their mouths: the Indus, Ganges, Yellow River, and many more.

Like most of them, the Yellow River in northern China not only suffers from considerable pollution and excessive water extraction, it also loses an ever greater share of its water because of a dramatically sinking water table in surrounding areas. Significantly more groundwater is being extracted from increasingly deep wells in the large basin of the lower Hai and Yellow Rivers with a total population of approximately 100 million people, including Beijing. Desertification as well as sand and dust storms are coming menacingly close to Beijing and other large cities from the parched fields and overgrazed steppes in the west and north of this large region. Thousands of villages have already been buried by the shifting sand, and millions of people have been driven away and left homeless.

I have already mentioned other examples of how seriously dwindling water resources will affect agriculture, and thus the world's food supply. Many more cases could be added. The consequence of this threatening situation can only be more careful utilization of this irreplaceable resource and effective prioritization of its use between agriculture and other sectors.

Even in many regions with average rainfall similar to that in Europe, irrigation has to be used much more sparingly because of the alternation between distinctive periods of rain and drought. Characteristic examples are the terraced rice paddies in many parts of Asia (Fig. 36), which are irrigated by a dense network of channels from a lake, river, or artificial basin and fertilized with alluvial deposits.

Figure 36 Terraced rice paddies in the Pokhara Valley in Nepal,
separated by low embankments for irrigation

In regions with little precipitation or water resources, specific low-loss (but capital-intensive) irrigation techniques will be increasingly used in the future. In countries like Cyprus and Israel more than half of the agricultural irrigation consists of these types of systems. Exact amounts of water are delivered directly to the plant's roots through the fine-tubing of drip-irrigation devices, similar to the ones often used in greenhouses. The reprocessing of wastewater and the desalinization of water from the oceans will also play an increasingly important role, whereby the costs and availability of energy will be crucial factors.

Energy as a Resource

There are strong regional differences in the consumption of energy for food production. The least amount of energy is used in developing countries by small farming families, who as subsistence farmers have access to neither the facilities nor the money to purchase pesticides, fertilizers, or mechanical aids. The largest amount of energy is consumed in industrialized countries, where all parts of the modern chain are applied to turn out high-quality processed food.

This chain begins with the high-tech propagation of seeds, mechanical soil preparation and automated seeding, and ends with the transport and (often deep-frozen) storage of the final product, which has again been processed using elaborate technological means. In between are the equally energy-intensive manufacture and motorized application of fertilizers and pesticides, a fully mechanical harvest, and one or more stages of intermediate storage, often including long-distance transport.

This consumption of energy contrasts with the potential contribution of agriculture to the production of energy. The largest and widely unused potential is in generating energy from the excess parts of crop plants in efficient incinerators. The production of "biofuels" and "biodiesel" from sugar cane, corn, and rapeseed is presently a much debated issue. In Brazil a significant share of the country's energy needs are now covered by ethanol produced from sugar cane, and in Europe rapeseed oil is being increasingly used (though in comparably small amounts) as fuel for diesel engines. "Renewable resources" are now grown, for instance, on more than 10% of Germany's agricultural land, and rapeseed oil accounts for several percent of all diesel fuel in the country.

This option, however, is as questionable as the provision of

increasing amounts of space for people to live or build transportation networks, factories, and leisure facilities, etc. (p. 201).
Producing a sufficient amount of food for a growing population
on less and less farmland is the harder to imagine, the more this
space is used for other purposes. Apart from that, the existing
problem of a global imbalance between influential centers of
agricultural production and those who are dependent on them
would become even larger.

Centers of Production and Centers of Demand

The world's most important centers of agricultural production
are Europe, the North American Midwest, the central and southeastern parts of South America, the east and the south of Australia, and large parts of Asia. With the exception of Asia, these
centers of production are also exporting centers for the most
important types of transportable and storable food and feed,
especially cereals, meat, and soybeans. For several decades Japan
was the major importing country, but China has now taken over
this position.

Set-aside programs in Europe and North America – introduced more for economic than for ecological reasons – have
created reserves of production that can be mobilized in emergency situations. To what extent the re-use of these areas for
farming would affect ecological interests is mainly a question of
the type of land use.

The situation is different in South America, particularly in
Brazil. Brazil replaced the United States as the major exporter of
soybeans at about the same time as China moved ahead of Japan
as the largest importer of wheat and soybeans. Superficially
speaking, Brazil could considerably strengthen this position and

become the largest exporter of wheat as well. In principle, additional land would be available for farming, but only at high economic and ecological risks.

Whether this potential is exploited or not is partially dependent on the development of prices and demand on the world market. Presently world market prices for soybeans and soy meal, which are based on yield per hectare and are fluctuating, are substantially higher than they are for wheat. One of Brazil's market advantages is its relatively low energy and labor costs compared to most industrialized countries.

From an ecological point of view, however, an extension of Brazilian agriculture at the cost of subtropical rainforests would very likely have catastrophic consequences. The particularly profitable cultivation of soybeans is largely concentrated in ecologically valuable, but easily eroded areas in the central Brazilian state of Mato Grosso. Cultivation continues to spread to the north into the adjacent Amazon region. This area is already greatly threatened as a result of state development measures and other forms of use – with unpredictable consequences for the climate and ecological stability.

The interplay of economic incentives and ecological consequences is highly complex, unpredictable, and therefore especially effective: Prices on the world market and conditions of production for soybeans and soy meal are currently so favorable that neither the costs for transport from the interior of Brazil, i.e. far from the coast, nor the low property prices and development costs play an important role; particularly since the construction of road and shipping networks has been massively funded by the government. Moreover, at least for the time being, there is a favorable subtropical climate with sufficient amounts of rainfall for above-average yields.

And thus we are witnesses of what a continuation of this

development will lead to: progressive deforestation of the rain-forests, a correspondingly high loss of biodiversity, soil erosion, regional and global climate change, a decline in productivity, and finally an ecological and economic collapse.

The economic damage could have just as big an influence on the global food situation as the ecological damage. The more South America develops into an important center for food and feed production and exports, similar to North America and Europe, the more dependent and endangered growing and hungry populations will be on the stability of this source.

Human history has always been marked by imbalances between those who produced food and raw materials on the one hand, and those who consumed and processed it on the other. The most well-known examples, albeit results of military conquests and economic exploitation, are North Africa and Western Europe as the "granaries" of Rome, and later the extra-European colonies as suppliers of food and raw materials to the European colonial powers.

The economic, political, and social consequences for the affected populations lasted for many generations and in part still prevail even today. They have often culminated in human catas-trophes such as deportation, collective forced labor, or the enslav-ing of entire peoples or ethnic groups. This even endured after the promulgation of individual rights of freedom for one's own priv-ileged citizens as a result of "enlightenment" and "humanism."

Regional imbalances between food production and consump-tion will always remain unavoidable, if only for climatic and ecological reasons. Making these imbalances as ecologically, economically, and socially acceptable as possible will be one of the most urgent tasks in the future. The twofold goal consists of preserving the climate and biosphere for sustainable agricultural production while at the same time creating humane general living conditions for everyone.

To achieve this goal, appropriate political measures (p. 236) are indispensable, but deep-seated customs, traditions, and cultural differences should not be disregarded.

Dietary Habits

In East Asia, smoked locusts, ants, and bees are considered nutritious and full of flavor; well-prepared bee and beetle maggots are even a delicacy. Most Europeans are disgusted at the very thought of this. Many of them, however, regard frog legs, snails, oysters, and squid as treats, which in turn arouse feelings of disgust elsewhere.

Various flavorings are added to European margarine products in accordance with the country to which they are to be shipped. In some Asian countries, for example, aromas are added to produce the rancid smell and taste so common there. We would reject the product as inedible.

Whether consciously or unconsciously, every person decides on whether food is attractive or not, enjoyable or inedible. This "organoleptic behavior" involves visual examination (color, consistency, and structure), smelling, and tasting, as well as reactions caused by cultural traditions, emotion, and instinct.

In view of this firmly anchored and seemingly irrational behavior, it should be of no surprise that in several African countries white corn or white sweet potatoes are seen as a welcome form of human nourishment while the yellow varieties serve as fodder. Highly nutritious yellow corn was even rejected by starving people when it was offered as part of an international aid program. Based on similar experience, the question remains open as to whether Golden Rice – despite its substantially improved quality – will be accepted by such cultures that have traditionally only known and accepted white rice as a form of food (p. 153).

Essentially the same applies to all kinds of meat and fish as well as to the different ways in which they are traditionally prepared. For most Europeans the consumption of dogs, cats, or rats is an unbearable thought, while elsewhere it is either a tradition or a question of survival.

Meat and fish are particularly important for another reason as well: The rapidly growing consumption of them has resulted in a great demand for feed and water, with grave consequences for the long-term guarantee of human sustenance.

Consumption of Meat and Fish

Approximately a third of agricultural land around the world is used for crop farming and two thirds is pastureland. By far the largest share of this pastureland consists of natural steppe vegetation in semi-arid areas with little precipitation. Just how poorly suited these areas are for growing crops was poignantly demonstrated by the failed attempts in Kazakhstan and several neighboring countries (p. 214).

For many millions of people the cattle, goat, and sheep herds on this barren, dry pastureland are the only source of food. However, these pastures are being increasingly threatened by overuse as a result of population growth. Rapidly spreading desertification in Nigeria (p. 218) and in northern China (p. 223) are two unmistakable examples of the constant danger of an ecological collapse – with corresponding and often deadly consequences for the affected populations.

This form of animal husbandry on natural pastures in

Figure 37 Intensive large-scale farming of young female turkeys in a
growing barn in Europe

numerous developing countries contrasts greatly with the practice in industrialized countries. Here most of the feed comes
from fields that are as fertile as those used for growing crops for

Figure 38 Intensive cattle farming in a multi-story stall in Japan

human consumption, and the majority of farm animals – especially cattle, pigs, and fowl – are not reared outside, in natural conditions, but in completely or partially automated, high-density pens (Figs. 37 and 38).

This type of intensive, large-scale livestock farming, compounded with the rapidly increasing consumption of meat, particularly in China and other developing and newly industrialized countries, has led to a total number and total weight of farm animals that greatly exceed the number and weight of the entire human population. In addition to forage grasses expressly developed for them, the animals are mainly fed corn, soy, wheat, and barley. A large part of the global wheat production and the predominant portion of the corn, soy, and barley production are used as fodder.

The more than 20 billion farm animals are an even greater burden for the Earth's biosphere than the 6 to 7 billion humans: through the direct or indirect displacement of countless other species; through the enormous amounts of agricultural land, water, energy, fertilizer, and pesticides used for the production of feed; through the amounts of water and energy needed for rearing the animals; through the vast amounts of excrement that leach into the soil and water; through the creation and spread of pathogens such as BSE and avian flu (as a result of the high-density animal populations) that affect not only animals, but potentially humans as well; and through the massive use of antibiotics in preventive and curative veterinary medicine.

The production of fodder for the generation of 1 kg of meat requires, depending on the type of animal, an area about three to ten times the size of that needed to produce 1 kg of wheat or rice for human consumption. This calculation does not include the enormous demand for water (at first for the fodder crops, and then for the animals) – despite dwindling water resources in many places (p. 222). Jeremy Rifkin and Josef Reichholf describe many additional aspects in their respective works *Beyond Beef: The Rise and Fall of the Cattle Culture* and *Der Tanz um das goldene Kalb* (The Dance Around the Golden Calf, no English-language publication).

In comparison with animals, water consumption and the feed conversion ratios are much more effective with most species of fish. The increase in fish production through aquaculture (artificial fish tanks, or enclosures in lakes, rivers, or the ocean) has been correspondingly rapid. The feed conversion of a balanced mixture of fodder with a proper portion of protein-rich soy meal is especially efficient. In the most favorable cases, 1–2 kg of feed results in 1 kg of fish weight.

By 2002 aquacultural fish production had grown to nearly half of that obtained from (strongly declining) commercial ocean fishing. More than two-thirds of this production was in China, which has an ancient tradition of this particularly efficient form of pisciculture (fish farming). In water-rich areas of Southeast Asia intensively irrigated fields are even used for rice and fish production at the same time.

Principally speaking, the same ecological and veterinary concerns that apply to meat production in densely populated stalls also applies to fish production in densely constructed aquatic enclosures, although with certain qualifications with regard to the amount of feed and water usage. By contrast, the value of meat, milk, dairy products, eggs, and fish as high quality nutritional fare rich in proteins, vitamins, essential fatty acids, and trace elements is undisputable (p. 90).

In the same way the steppe people mainly or solely live on meat and milk from their herds, many coastal dwellers depend on catching fish. But their fishing grounds are just as threatened by overfishing as the pastures of those pastoral peoples are by overgrazing. In this case, however, it is not only the coastal dwellers themselves who are exploiting their fishing grounds, but instead fleets of commercial fishing vessels from a worldwide industry that has decimated many stocks of fish to the point of extinction.

Coincident with the Green Revolution (between 1950 and 1990), the harvesting of saltwater fish increased almost fivefold to over 80 million tons per year. This amount was almost twice as high as the production of beef. The stocks of many species of edible fish have since declined over 90%. A targeted recovery of fish populations will at least temporarily lead to a further decline in the harvesting of saltwater fish.

As with vegetative food production, the only solution for meat and fish production consists of assigning ecological sustainability a higher priority than questions of indulgence and status. And this certainly has to be the case when ecological reality only allows for a sufficient and secure amount of food for humans through restrictions on meat, milk, and fish production in favor of vegetative sources of food.

However, there is considerable resistance to this in many cultures. It can only be slowly overcome because it is to a large extent emotionally or economically fixed with engrained eating habits, directly through meat consumption due to conviction or social prestige, or indirectly through economic means of existence or financial advantages from subsidized exports or cheap imports. Actually changing these habits will probably depend on the harshness of the dictates of reality. Ultimately, giving up a custom has always been more a question of having to than merely being able to, or even wanting to.

But even if everyone was completely successful in contributing one's share, it would still be little more than a drop in the bucket compared to the vast size of the task – a long-term and secure supply of food for a *growing* population. Whatever form a workable solution ends up taking, it has to be prepared, supported and put into action by way of effective political decisions at a national and international level.

Political Decisions

At least in democratic systems important political decisions are based on social acceptance and the public opinion of the majority (p. 191). It is therefore all the more important that politics and society become aware of the overriding significance and urgency of adopting effective measures.

In the following summary of the most important demands I refer once again to the CGIAR consultative group (p. 209) and to their detailed rationale and explanations in *The Doubly Green Revolution*. This committee of experts explicitly emphasizes the magnitude of the challenge and the essential importance of each individual demand, which can be wholly effective only if all other demands are met concurrently:

- an economic policy which does not discriminate against agriculture;
- liberalization of the world market for all agricultural consumer goods and products;
- effective financing mechanisms that give small farmers in remote regions access to loans, deposits, and services for marketing their products;
- land reform or reallocation where necessary;
- an appropriate infrastructure in rural regions, including water supply, transport, and marketing;

- investments in education, health, family planning, a supply of clean water and information about healthy nutrition;
- improvements in the roles and rights of women, ethnic groups and other minorities;
- development or improvement and dissemination of appropriate cultivation methods in cooperation with local farmers.

The first two demands concern industrialized countries as much as developing countries. All other demands essentially refer to developing countries, but require either the direct (through the reorientation of development aid) or indirect (through example and support) assistance of industrialized nations.

All too often industrialized countries fail to see that the former phase of colonialism has been replaced with a new and barely less development-inhibiting form of economic dependence for many developing countries. It would also have fatal consequences for the industrialized countries themselves if they did not understand the global political, demographic, economic, ecological, and social effects of the continuing population growth and environmental destruction, and the simultaneously widening gap between poverty and affluence as an urgent request for immediate action.

However, to be credible and successful in everyday practice, all political decisions have to be accompanied by additional and very fundamental measures:

- an effective fight against corruption, mismanagement, and waste both inside and outside our own realm;
- an improvement in the general basic knowledge of, and the ability to make well-founded judgments about, ecological relationships;

- instruction of the general public with regard to measures
  and aspirations that are both free of ideology and
  task-oriented;
- recognition and appreciation of different traditions, cultural
  values, and setting of priorities.

The seeming utopia of these demands underscores the magnitude of the task. But it is not universal human dignity alone that should provide the necessary focus on the challenges for politics and society at large, but the industrialized countries' own interest in a stable and secure global situation as well. The re-determination of government aid programs as a way of helping people to help themselves has to be a major part of this task.

Helping People to Help Themselves

The commonly employed expression "helping people to help themselves" actually addresses two sides of the same coin. On the one hand it demands renunciation of decision-making dominance on the part of the contributor with regard to the manner in which resources are used (or compensated for) by the recipient, and on the other hand the transformation from dependence to self-determined action, with the common goal of establishing a true, mutually beneficial partnership.

This revised form of help consists of several largely independent components. Especially extensive measures are government-run mid-term or long-term developmental aid programs, government-funded ad hoc programs in emergency situations, and numerous privately supported programs of non-governmental (often international) organizations, which are usually less bureaucratic and therefore particularly flexible. This latter group is an especially good example of a purely altruistic and most effective way of helping people to help themselves. With regard to improved food supplies in developing countries, there is also another effective and intensive form of helping people to help themselves in the areas of education, research, and application. Countless long-term development aid projects have been planned and carried out as a result of individual collaborations between scientists from industrial and developing countries, often with the support of private foundations.

I have already stressed the leading role of the Rockefeller and Ford Foundations in the breeding of corn, wheat, and rice varieties as a prerequisite for the Green Revolution (p. 206), as well as the significant contributions of these and the Gates Foundation to the development of Golden Rice and ProVitaMinRice (p. 153). Besides these large and well-known foundations, there are many others specifically supporting research projects aimed at improving the food supply in developing countries.

A concrete example of a major personal donation in Germany is the *Vater und Sohn Eiselen Foundation* in Ulm. For more than 20 years this purely private foundation has supported research projects, symposia, and educational scholarships on the "generation of knowledge and its application to reduce hunger and poverty in the world." The largest single contribution was made for a research project entitled "Biotechnology and Plant Breeding – Applied Genetics for the Improvement of World Nutrition." This long-term cooperative project was carried out between the University of Hohenheim and numerous research groups in developing countries.

The importance of such foundations goes far beyond financial assistance alone. They draw public attention to problems, offer approaches to solving problems, initiate projects and provide an impetus for further financing, and mediate partnerships and exchange of experience. Additionally, they establish connections between science, economics, politics, the media, and the public. And even more importantly, foundations are role models and symbols of the fact that significant action is most likely to occur when the combination of private initiative, the sharing of material wealth, and personal responsibility point the way.

Progress through Solidarity

Excessive population growth and an extravagant way of dealing with nearly all accessible resources have characterized our behavior up to now. Abundance fosters extravagance. If moderation is lacking, progress is falsely equated with growth and proliferation, and their absence is even considered to be a loss.

Economic growth, capital growth, and increases in productivity, sales, sporting success, and personal performance of all kinds are public and private goals in almost all areas, with corresponding consequences for those that do not keep up. Population growth and the extension of territory and power as age-old goals for groups, peoples, and entire countries have served as inducements and examples for individuals. Now they are examples of the principal impossibility of continued growth and unlimited propagation.

The inevitability of progress (in the literal sense of putting one step in front of another, see p. 13) forces us to undertake effective countermeasures. If quantity and growth can no longer be the goal, they have to be replaced with quality and innovative improvements. Sacrifice thus becomes a sign of quality: If we take our priorities for the future as the measure of progress, and for the sake of our environment, our diet, and our health do without all the things that undermine these priorities, then we will automatically discover those new developments and innovations for which we can and must assume responsibility and which irresponsible risks we have to avoid.

Summary

The sustainable securing of food for all humans requires a drastic change in our dealing with natural resources, as well as the elimination of hunger and poverty as the main causes of the continuing population growth. Agricultural productivity can be significantly enhanced, especially in developing countries, through improvements in breeding methods, farming technology, and the global sociopolitical, economic, and infrastructural conditions. On the other hand, this productivity is increasingly threatened by climate change, ecological damage, desertification, and dwindling water resources. Considerable food reserves would become available through a reduction in intensive livestock farming in favor of cultivating cereal crops, fruit, and vegetables for direct human consumption.

All these upcoming measures require radical and effective political decisions at both the national and international levels. Indispensable prerequisites include improved general knowledge and objective factual instruction of the public, economic and political sectors about the global ecological and economic consequences of biodiversity losses and global warming as well as their effects on food production, the availability of natural resources, and population growth.

Development aid programs offered by industrialized

countries will best serve the long-term common interests of both industrialized and developing nations if they promote self-initiative, educational standards, and cooperative partnership by helping people to help themselves. Valuable additional help is provided by non-governmental aid organizations, private foundations, personal commitment and individual contacts. The overall goal is the replacement of quantitative growth and the overuse of natural resources with qualitative progress in all spheres of life.

9 Conclusions for Practical Realization

The outline presented here of an extremely complex subject cannot be any more than a mere stressing of core themes within the given framework. And this can certainly be no different with regard to realistic conclusions which have to be based on universally valid requirements: they must respect our basic existential needs, correspond to our ethical standards, be in accord with scientific knowledge, and be practicable under the existing circumstances. Together, these requirements call for an orientation toward ethically and practically motivated priorities.

Orientation on Primary Goals

A ranking of priorities of even the most important orienting criteria cannot be completely unequivocal in every respect. It will depend, for instance, on how individual persons react to an emergency; on whether they place greater value on their own lives or on humanity and the biosphere as a whole.

Because the outcome of such a decision is at the very least uncertain, it should be avoided if at all possible. This would allow for the dignity – including the possibility of survival – of the individual to be ranked below that of humanity as a whole without violating individual dignity. Once this is achieved, a ranking of priorities would be as follows (including the practical integration of genetic engineering):

1. Preservation of a viable biosphere – for its own sake as well as that of humankind – including the necessary quality of air, water, and soil as well as sufficient amounts of space for healthy living conditions;
2. human nourishment (quantity and quality);
3. human health (prevention and healing);
4. respect for all additional aspects of human dignity;
5. species conservation (including improvements in animal welfare and the definition of breeding goals and limits).

Such priority ranking demands that every precedent goal is superior to the following one, and conversely, that each succeeding goal has to be subordinate to those preceding it. But every goal is still of outstanding – if only relative – importance and if at all possible should not be invalidated by a preceding goal. That this is not always practicable and can lead to serious problems is clearly evident in the many conflicts, e.g. between modern medical care and human dignity or environmental protection and human nutrition.

This ambivalence is certainly no reason to abstain from doing whatever is necessary. For those who are aware of this inescapability, the only solution is to compare and analyze the available possibilities, deduce practicable decisions and take appropriate action.

The discourse up to this point should have clarified the relative importance of the first four criteria. The last criterion (species conservation in the widest sense), by contrast, is neither clearly defined nor biologically or ethically easy to comprehend, particularly as it is greatly restricted by the superordinate goal of providing human nutrition. The conflict between environmental protection and human overpopulation and nutrition is once again very apparent. Environmental protection is not only an independent goal in its own right (protection of species and population sizes), but is also an element of the most important and overriding goal of all: the preservation of a viable biosphere that provides appropriate conditions for human life.

Species protection, as long as it is not by itself an integral part of protecting the biosphere as a whole, has two different aspects: the greatest possible protection of all uncultivated species from deliberate or accidental genetic modification by humans, and improved protection of animals for ethical reasons. Both aspects have to do with genetic engineering, either directly or indirectly. This is why it is important to clarify the scope of this protection before a long-term decision is conducted about the use of genetic engineering in those areas in question. However, as genetic engineering in crop plant breeding is less affected by this reflection, I will limit my comments to the following brief discourse.

Extended Protection of Species

Except for the breeding of large animals (cattle, horses, pigs, or sheep, etc.), which is regulated by law, the breeding of animals, plants, and microorganisms using conventional methods is open to everyone, as long as all relevant regulations are observed, particularly animal protection laws and rules for dealing with pathogens. The commonly known results of this type of breeding are not only all kinds of farm animals and crops, and all microorganisms put to biotechnological use, but the majority of our domestic pets and ornamental plants as well. Examples of the arbitrariness of limits in these areas of breeding are numerous breeds of dog with extreme peculiarities ranging from an almost complete lack of hair, blindness, and an incapability of movement to pronounced aggressiveness.

The intensive livestock farming for meat, dairy, and egg production and the corresponding breeding goals have been heavily criticized by animal welfare and conservationist organizations as well as by many individuals in a less organized form. As in most other areas, however, the behavior of customers largely determines the prevailing practice.

Dog breeding and intensive livestock farming with the respective breeding practices are only indications that the goals and limits of any breeding should be re-evaluated and strictly regulated independently of the form of animal keeping. Only then will it be possible to compare the results of different *breeding methods* (conventional crossing, artificial insemination, the cloning of multiple copies, and genetic engineering) and to adopt limits or even complete bans for certain *breeding products*. The incorrect equating of genetic engineering with artificial insemination through "embryo technology" or with cloning in "animal surrogate mothers" will be used as an emotionally provocative argument as long as ethically questionable breeding results and corresponding forms of animal keeping dominate and encumber the discussion.

Even if an ethical component is essentially insignificant in traditional plant breeding, the possibilities of genetic engineering nevertheless raise ethical questions here as well. This pertains to the open question in Chapter 7 about the right to modify a genotype beyond cross-breeding and hybridization barriers. Although there are already numerous legal test cases with genetic engineering (p. 135ff.) and without (p. 113), they alone cannot serve as justification for the further course of action.

In my opinion, if we really want to take environmental

protection and the preservation of nature seriously, we have to define clear limits of human intervention in the evolution of species. In this respect, comprehensive species conservation is vital. The following should therefore apply with regard to genetic engineering:

> The practical use of genetic engineering – but not basic research in molecular biology – should remain limited to organisms that are subject to breeding by other methods as well. Whether genetic engineering should actually be used in a particular case should be decided in accordance with the criteria and goals listed above.

Plant Genetic Engineering

If the goals and limits of crop plant breeding are fundamentally determined or remain deliberately undetermined, then the application of genetic engineering should continue to be an option. In line with the suggested ranking of priorities, which provide food for all people and simultaneously protect the biosphere, or at least do no harm to it. This includes every breeding goal that directly or indirectly:

- prevents further expansion of agriculture or reduces it in ecologically sensitive areas in favor of environmental protection;
- reduces or eliminates the pollution of air, water, and soil with substances that are hazardous to either humans or the environment;
- results in increased food production;
- improves nutritional quality.

The advantages and disadvantages of each measure that might help to meet one of these goals have to be individually and carefully considered in accordance with the aforementioned priority criteria. In so doing, subordinate goals should also be considered (as much as possible) in the order of their relative importance.

The fact that every decision – regardless of its ramifications – has to be a judgment call due to a lack of absolute criteria is nothing new and finds universal application. Nevertheless, we are particularly conscious of this dilemma when new technological possibilities call for a correspondingly higher degree of responsibility.

And thus it becomes clear that the application or non-application of more or less far-reaching possibilities of genetic engineering can only be a judgment call as well, made on the basis of weighed requirements. After all, the possibilities range from the transfer of a single gene from the same species, which merely corresponds to a greatly distilled conventional breeding procedure, up to an innovative combination of genes which never occurred before in that organism.

Those who prefer a different ranking order will perhaps reach a different decision about the application or non-application of genetic engineering. In my opinion there is only one possible order of the five most important criteria (p. 244), and this leads to an unambiguous conclusion:

> Plant genetic engineering, without any methodological
> restrictions, should be used for the breeding of crops if this
> serves to protect the biosphere or to provide sufficient amounts
> of food for all people more efficiently than other available and
> acceptable methods. In doing so, and in addition to preserving
> a viable biosphere, the protection of other species (wild types)
> from genetic modifications has to be ensured as much as the

superordinate criteria allow. As a rule, the product and not the method of breeding should be evaluated.

If these conclusions and their rationale are to form the basis for a generally valid procedure, then they also have to pertain to all other areas where genetic engineering might be applied. Thus they also require that:

- genetic engineering not be used with humans, at least for the time being, i.e. with the goal of hereditary genetic modifications of the germline (p. 183);
- genetic engineering for human health, especially using laboratory organisms, only be applied to the extent that the superordinate criteria are not violated;
- the use of genetic engineering for the breeding of beneficial and ornamental organisms (except for crops) – including domestic pets – be either prohibited or at least strictly limited to the scope allowed within the ranking of priorities (no specific ranking is made here, as there is no necessity within the scope of this book);
- genetic engineering not be used with all other organisms, unless for research purposes in accordance with relevant regulations, or in special cases where the predefined goals make this desirable.

Guidelines and Laws

Molecular biology and genetic engineering are subject to specific guidelines, regulations, laws, and statutory instruments in the same manner as the handling of other materials and techniques: chemicals, flammable material, biological organisms, radioactive substances, x-ray devices, electricity, radio frequencies, etc. In most countries the regulations related to genetic engineering are derived from the self-imposed rules that molecular biologists had initially agreed to (p. 190). They differ very little among comparable research-oriented industrialized countries, except for the regulations dealing with field tests and agricultural usage, which again vary in their degree of stringency.

The uniformity of genetic engineering laws and regulations and their enactment within the European Union has not been resolved up to now (2008). The "release" and the commercial cultivation of transgenic plants are not only dealt with in different ways, but are assessed differently by the general public as well. The obvious determining factors of the compromise-based EU policies are, apart from the major role of public opinion, European trade and business interests, especially in developing nations.

By the time the first controlled field test of a genetically modified petunia was being accompanied by public protests in Germany in the summer of 1990, more than one hundred similar tests had already been conducted around the world, most of them in the United States, France, Canada, and Belgium. Soon afterwards transgenic plants were licensed as approved cultivars in several countries outside Europe and planted in rapidly increasing amounts (p. 20).

On the one hand, research in plant molecular biology serves both of the two highest goals: environmental protection and human nutrition; but on the other hand it should, wherever possible, not run counter to the similarly important and closely related goal of increased species conservation. For this reason, species in the wild should be protected as much as possible from inadvertent transfer of an engineered gene modification. This "biological safety" issue and its strict observance is an extremely controversial, scientifically unsolved problem which can only be clarified through further unbiased and goal-oriented research.

Until recently, the extent to which genes are naturally exchanged among species ("horizontal gene transfer") has not been verifiable through direct means and could only be indirectly derived from the extent of crossings or hybridizations. A conclusive answer to this question can only be obtained using molecular biological methods. Thus it will be important to carry out further research and thoroughly observe transgenic plants in parallel with supposedly receptive wild types. Well-founded statements about this issue will not be possible until scientifically reliable results from this type of "biological safety research" are available. And only then will we be in the position to draw relevant conclusions with regard to practical application.

We can expect that most of our main food plants, which are only able to survive under intensive management practices, will not spread in an uncontrolled fashion. Their further optimization with the help of genetic engineering methods should only serve the three most important criteria. This expressly includes – as opposed to basic research – cultivation outside biological security zones. A gradual transition from controlled laboratory conditions to greenhouse and field tests must precede this final step, however, and the chances and risks have to be evaluated or estimated at each step.

Every new variety of a food plant, whether developed with conventional breeding techniques or genetic engineering methods will only be approved and licensed for commercial use upon successful completion of a state-certified test. This includes a thorough investigation of its nutritional quality and other characteristics important to consumers. The combination of this testing procedure with a step-by-step decision on the breeding method would allow for a *product-oriented* application of genetic engineering under the following conditions:

The approval of a genetic engineering procedure for crop plant breeding will be decided on a case basis. The prerequisite is a positive appraisal of foreseeable chances of success at each step on the basis of the priority ranking. The evaluation of the product in accordance with specified criteria will determine its market release.

Measures in Other Areas

Qualitative progress in the breeding of food plants should help to solve the ongoing conflict between destruction of the environment and food production. The reason for primarily searching for a solution in the field of agriculture is not that environmental problems would then be solved. However, securing human sustenance is of the highest priority after protection of the biosphere. Both of these goals are imperative, but require many additional efforts beyond the scope of plant breeding.

Plant breeding alone cannot save our endangered environment.

Every additional measure for saving a viable biosphere opens up just as many interrelated questions as the breeding of agricultural crops does. I therefore have to limit myself to essential core demands.

The most important measures are the ending of population growth, effective environmental protection, and a social and economic adjustment between the wealthy and the poor.

Effective environmental protection demands that nature is not only protected for the sake of our living conditions, but above all for its own sake. This calls for more than merely maintaining the biosphere at the limit of its viability, or parceling and devaluating nature reserves for the sake of special interests to the point that such make-believe areas become more of a detriment than a benefit.

Effective environmental protection and nature conservation require that a majority of people have a corresponding consciousness and basic attitude. The environment begins for every one of us in our immediate surroundings. People showing others just how seriously they take environmental protection themselves will achieve a great deal more than those who spend their lives anxiously demanding action from, "those at the top" only to realize in the end that they have lost everything, even the valuable time to do something themselves. "Those at the top" are all of us, though indirectly (p. 172). The saying applies here as everywhere: He who attempts to change a person for the better by setting a good example thus changes two.

The necessity of a less intensive form of agriculture and several additional measures have already been discussed in Chapter 1. In the political, economic, and social sectors the greatest challenge will be the elimination of the "North-South divide," without which a solution to population and environmental problems is unimaginable. Stopping environmental pollution and the overuse of resources in industrialized countries will be a comparatively easy preparatory exercise.

There is hardly an area in which the increasingly questionable *quantitative* achievements of growth and aggrandizement as well as the conquering and wasting of resources must not be replaced by *qualitative* progress. Among these are all forms of unrestrained consumption, ranging from fashionable "consumer goods" and the destruction of nature through tourism to the daily sensationalist reporting and ideological seductions.

"There are three kinds of enchantment" according to the

modern fairy tale *In the Kingdom of Mescal*, "dazzling brilliance, arousing desires on the market of dreams, and frightening someone with empty words." Frustration and "no future" are still among the timid answers.

Bread and Circuses

"Daily bread" stands for our food, i.e. for an essential human need. The question of how we can bring this need into the greatest possible harmony with the natural world that surrounds and sustains us is the subject of this book. By posing this question we realize just how much we are part of this natural world, under whose terms and challenges our own biological and cultural evolution has taken place in interaction with all other parts.

Bread is not the only human need. The Roman emperors promised their citizens *panem et circenses* (bread and circuses). They knew they would lose favor with their people if they were not able to satisfy both needs. Just as bread symbolizes our physical needs, circuses, or games and entertainment, stand for the emotional ones.

We should not underestimate the demanding power of emotional needs. They appear in such widely different forms as the educational games of children, the intellectual games of scientists, "games of chance," and games as rest and relaxation in compensation for product-oriented work. In each of these forms there is a satisfying of needs, which as the "free interplay of powers" are at least subjectively considered to be purposeless. *Homo sapiens* is not only working *homo faber*, but also game-playing *homo ludens*.

A child's play instinct is its innate drive to learn, to personally develop, and to investigate and conquer its environment to

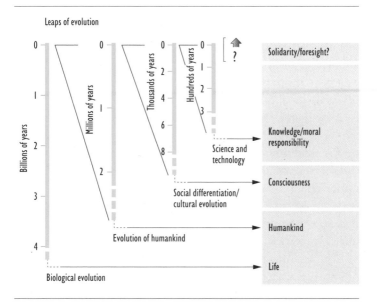

Figure 39 Schematic illustration of the continuously decreasing periods of time in which the different stages of human evolution have occurred

The arrow on the upper right indicates the current critical phase within which the conflict between excessive human population growth and the carrying capacity of the biosphere has to be solved. The question mark indicates the uncertainness of future development.

the point where it realizes and respects the boundaries – a nearly perfect analogy of the species *Homo sapiens* as a whole.

This is another important aspect of the turning point at which we now stand. Bread is one aspect, and play is the other. Both of them have reached their natural boundaries, both require a change of course from quantity to quality. Our play with nature must also change. We have reached the point from which we can no longer explore the boundaries as part of the old game, but rather their fundamental nature as part of a new one: the exploration of effective protection measures. Understanding humans and nature as an unrestricted but vulnerable entity corresponds exactly to the present state of our cultural development in an age of science and technology.

As with every earlier generation we, those who are now alive, are the heirs of the previous development. We are not responsible for the condition of our heritage, but we are fully responsible for the way we administer it and the shape in which we pass it on to our own heirs. And this is the unusual aspect of our inheritance: for the first time in the history of human evolution, the time period for an unavoidable change of course has been reduced to our very own lifetimes (Fig. 39).

The previous course was to investigate the boundaries and limits of growth, power, and consumption. The new course must be determined by solidarity and foresight.

Summary

The technological application of scientific knowledge has to respect the priorities of established ethical criteria. Absolute priority has to consist in securing the existence of humans and their environment. This requires a fundamental change in the use of natural resources, including an ecologically acceptable and at the same time highly productive form of agriculture.

To the extent that genetic engineering is able to serve as an aid to plant breeding, it should be applied as long as it proves advantageous in accordance with at least one of following five principal criteria without entailing disadvantages for the respective superordinate: 1. Preservation of a viable biosphere, 2. A sufficient quantity and quality of human nourishment, 3. Human health in general (prevention and healing), 4. Respect for all additional aspects of human dignity, and 5. Extended species conservation.

Without complementary measures in other areas, increased yield and an improved quality of food plants will not solve the conflict between human sustenance and the threatened biosphere. Improved food production must be accompanied by qualitative progress in changing our lifestyles, particularly through an effective and sustainable form of environmental protection, a rapid curtailment of population growth, and a lasting social and economic adjustment between wealth and poverty, power and powerlessness, access and a lack of availability.

Afterword

The challenge is as great as it is new. Establishing is always easier than economizing and dispensing with accessible goals. The long history of humankind has been characterized by growth through the conquest of living space, multiplication, and the elimination of external threats. There were no more important goals than these. And now, within just a few decades, these same goals have been completely inverted. Suddenly there is no more urgent task than to end population growth and to renounce our own threats to a severely limited biosphere whose healthy spheres are shrinking before our eyes.

One of the key global problems is to link high agricultural productivity with sustainable environmental protection. To what extent genetic engineering can contribute to the solution of this particularly urgent and difficult task is yet unknown. My basic attitude, which is cautiously optimistic, has surely been discernible. But first we have to decide on the goals and limits for exploiting the potential of genetic engineering. The more well-founded our position on this option is, the more responsible our actions will be. Those who endorse genetic engineering must understand what they are doing – and the same principle applies to those who reject it.

Genetic engineering has played a prominent role in this book due to its novelty and its revolutionary possibilities. It was never my intention, however, to advertise genetic engineering. It needs no advertisement. It is not a manufactured commercial product, but is a technology that is available if required. What genetic engineering needs is an unbiased evaluation of its advantages and disadvantages. Everyone can contribute to this through their own efforts. And yet, this book is indeed intended to be an advertisement. It aims to advertise a more conscious and responsible way of dealing with nature and with ourselves. Instead of wastefully destroying nature with technological means, we should apply all useful forms of technology with moderation in order to help preserve it. The question is no longer whether we are allowed to interfere with the natural evolution of species (or with creation). We have done this very effectively for a long time. The decisive question is rather: How do we preserve a viable diversity of creatures – including ourselves – and a world worth living in?

The bite taken in the apple from the Tree of Knowledge occurred long ago. The next great breakthrough to individual self-knowledge in classical antiquity culminated in the famous temple inscription "Know thyself." The consummation of this knowledge by extending from the self to all fellow human beings was the exhortation to "Love your neighbor as thyself." This form of self-knowledge has now been deepened further and extended to our whole environment. We realize that the inner circle includes all life.

Our cultural development is unstoppable and irreversible, just like the time in which it progresses. With knowledge grows responsibility, and with the possibilities of action, the personal freedom of decision. We have become increasingly free to decide on our own responsible actions.

By asking the question of whether and for how long our planet can still feed its people, we are recognizing our responsibility.

We have a great deal to lose and a great deal to gain.

Glossary

amino acid sequence: Sequence of amino acids that determines the structure of *proteins* (amino acid polymers).

bactericide: A substance that kills bacteria.

biosphere: The area of the Earth that contains life.

biotope: An area that supports a distinct community.

biocoenosis: Community of organisms inhabiting a biotope.

callus: Tissue growth originating from wounds, cell aggregates or single cells.

cell suspension culture: Single cells or cell aggregates cultivated in a liquid nutrient medium.

chromosome: Large molecule which carries up to thousands of genes. The complete set of genes (the *genome*) is located on an organism-specific number of chromosomes (humans have 2 x 23).

clone: A genetically identical descendent of a cell, a piece of tissue or an organism.

cross-breeding: Breeding by crossing genetically distinct individuals from the same species.

cultivar: A cultivated plant *variety*, selected for its desirable traits.

DNA: Deoxyribonucleic acid, a linear chain molecule composed of four different types of deoxyribonucleotide.

domestication: The transformation of wild forms of crop plants or animals through target-oriented breeding.

enzyme: Catalyst (increases the rate) of a specific reaction in cell metabolism.

fungicide: A substance that kills fungi.

gene: A single hereditary unit that determines or co-determines a particular trait of an organism.

gene bank: Collection of seeds from wild-type and cultivated varieties of plants that are of interest to breeders or conservationists.

genome: The complete package of an organism's genetic material.

genotype: The entire genetic identity of an individual.

germ cell: Sexual cell (egg cell, sperm cell or pollen).

habitat: The environment where a plant or animal normally lives or occurs.

herbicide: A substance that kills plants.

hybrid: The result of crossing different species. Hybrids capable of reproduction are rare among animals and more common with plants. The formation of hybrids is prevented to a great extent by natural hybridization barriers.

hybridization: Formation of hybrids.

hybrid variety: The result of crossing inbred lines to create more productive, mostly sterile plants.

insecticide: A substance that kills insects.

monogenic: Determined by one gene.

monogerm seed: Seed with a single ovule per fruit.

mutagen: A chemical or physical agent that changes the genetic constitution of an organism.

mutant: A genetically altered individual resulting from a mutation.

mutation: A genetic alteration.

mycorrhiza: A symbiotic association between a fungus and a plant root.

mycotoxin: A poison produced by a fungus.

nitrogen fixation: The transformation of atmospheric nitrogen into a biologically useful form.

pathogen: An agent that causes disease.

phenotype: The observed appearance of an organism, due to its genotype as well as its environment.

photosynthesis: The formation of organic substances from carbon dioxide and water using light as the energy source.

plasticity: The adaptability of an organism to respective environmental conditions, synonymous with adaptive modification.

Polygenic: Determined by several genes.

protein: A linear chain molecule containing 20 different types of amino acids which are joined together in a sequence specified by the responsible gene

promotor: A control element regulating the expression of a gene as specified by intracellular signal molecules.

protoplast: A cell which has lost its wall, but is otherwise complete, i.e. surrounded by a plasma membrane.

resistance: The ability to withstand a biological stress factor, e.g. a pathogen or insect herbivore.

restriction enzyme: An enzyme which cuts through genes at specific recognition sites.

somatic (= body) cell: Any type of cell of an organism except germ cells.

structural gene: The part of a gene that encodes a specific product.

tissue culture: Tissue cultivated in a controlled environment on a solid substrate or in liquid suspension.

tolerance: The ability to withstand a non-biological stressor, e.g. an herbicide or heavy metal ions.

transgene: A gene that has been transferred from one organism to another through genetic engineering.

variability: Changeability of the genetic constitution of individuals from the same species; the ability to deviate from the average *genotype* of a species.

variety: The particular genotype of a species, with cultivated forms of crops also known as *cultivar*.

virulent: Active as a pathogen.

virus: A potentially pathogenic, incomplete biological entity, as opposed to bacteria and fungi, that is dependent on a live host organism for reproduction.

References and Recommendations for Further Reading

Bold type indicates specially recommended information that is supplemental to this book's principal topics.

Al-Babili, Salim, and Peter Beyer. 2005. *Golden Rice–five years on the road–five years to go? TRENDS in Plant Science* 10:565–573.

Allard, Robert W. 1999. *Principals of Plant Breeding.* New York: John Wiley.

Braun, Joachim von. 2005. *The World Food Situation. An Overview.* Washington: International Food Policy Institute (www.ifpri.org).

ASSINSEL, ed. 2000. *Nahrung für 5000 Millionen.* Nyon, Switzerland: Internationale Vereinigung der Pflanzenzüchter.

Brown, Lester R. 2004. *Outgrowing the Earth. The food security challenge in an age of falling water tables and rising temperatures.* **New York: Norton & Co.**

Buber, Martin. 1978. *Zwiesprache: Traktat vom dialogischen Leben.* Heidelberg: Lambert Schneider:37.

Cohen, Joel I. 2005. *Poorer nations turn to publicly developed GM crops. Nature Biotechnology* 23:27–33.

Conway, Gordon. 1997. *The Doubly Green Revolution. Food for all in the 21st century.* **London: Penguin Books.**

Deutsche Gesellschaft für die Vereinten Nationen, eds. 2005. *Kurzfassung des Berichts über die menschliche Entwicklung 2005*. Berlin.

Diamond, Jared. 2005. *Guns, Germs and Steel: The Fates of Human Societies*. **New York: W. W. Norton.**

Evans, Lloyd T. 1998. *Feeding the Ten Billion. Plants and population growth*, **Cambridge: Cambridge University Press.**

Food and Agriculture Organization (FAO). Rome, www.fao. org.

Gonsalves, Dennis. 2004. *Transgenic Papaya in Hawaii and Beyond*. *AgBioForum* 7 (1 & 2):36–40.

International Food Policy Research Institute (IFPRI). Washington, www.ifpri.org.

James, Clive. 2004 and 2007. *Global Status of Commercialized Biotech/ GM Crops. ISAAA Briefs No. 32 and 37. International Service for the Acquisition of Agri-biotech Applications*. Ithaca, NY.

Jonas, Hans. 1985. *Technik, Medizin und Ethik*. Frankfurt: Insel.

Kaufmann, Stefan H. E. 2009. *The New Plagues: Pandemics and Poverty in a Globalized World*. **London: Haus Publishing**

Mauser, Wolfram. 2009. *Water Resources: Efficient, Sustainable and Equitable Use*. **London: Haus Publishing**

Latif, Mojib. 2009. *Climate Change: The Point of No Return*. **London: Haus Publishing**

Meyers Großes Taschenlexikon. 1987. Mannheim/Wien/Zürich: B. I. Taschenbuchverlag.

Nietzsche, Friedrich. 1969. *Thus Spoke Zarathustra*, London: Penguin Classics.

Ortega y Gasset, José. 1994. *The Revolt of the Masses*. New York: W.W. Norton.

Qaim, Matin, and Ira Matuschke. 2005. *Impacts of genetically modified crops in developing countries: a survey. Quarterly Journal of International Agriculture* 44:207–227.

Reichholf, Josef H. 2009. *The Demise of Diversity: Loss and Extinction.* **London: Haus Publishing**

Reichholf, Josef H. 2006. *Der Tanz um das goldene Kalb. Der Ökokolonialismus Europas.* Berlin: Wagenbach.

Rifkin, Jeremy. 1992. *Beyond Beef: The Rise and Fall of the Cattle Culture.* E.P. Dutton.

Schäfer, Georg, and Nan Cuz. 1970. *In the Kingdom of Mescal.* Berkeley: Shambala.

Vergil, Publius Maro. 1961. *Georgica*, Zurich: Artemis: 171–185.

Wambugu, Florence. 1999. *Why Africa needs agricultural biotech. Nature* 400:15–16.

World Bank: http://www.worldbank.org.

Wilson, Edward O. 1999. *The Diversity of Life.* **New York: W.W. Norton.**

Wilson, Edward O. 2002. *The Future of Life.* **New York: Knopf.**

Picture credits

All graphics and maps: Peter Palm, Berlin; Fig. 2: Regierungspräsidium Münster; Fig. 4: Archiv für Kunst und Geschichte, Berlin; Fig. 5: Archaeological Museum, Teheran; Figs. 7 and 8: Iraq Museum, Baghdad; Fig. 9: *Das alte Ägypten*, Holle-Verlag, Baden-Baden; Fig. 10: Albertinum, Dresden; Fig. 11: Mainfränkisches Museum, Würzburg; Fig. 13: Camille Flammarion: *Meteorologie populaire*, Paris 1888; Fig. 14: Munch Museum, Oslo; Fig. 15: Musée de Poche, Paris; Figs. 16, 17, 24, 25: Frauke Furkert, Cologne; Figs. 18, 21: ASSINSEL, Amsterdam; Figs. 20, 22, 26, 27, 29, 30: Max Planck Institute for Plant Breeding Research, Cologne; Fig. 23: Kleinwanzlebener Saatzucht, Einbeck; Fig. 28: Peter Beyer, Freiburg; Fig. 31: Dennis Gonsalves, Hawaii; Fig. 32: Human Development Report 2005; Figs. 33, 34, 36, 38: Yann Arthur-Bertrand; Figs. 35: Myers et al.: *Nature* 403, pp. 853–858, 2000.

As it was not possible to determine or contact all entitled persons despite extensive effort, the publisher is under obligation to remunerate any subsequently asserted legal claims in accordance with customary fee schedules.